WOODCARVING BASICS

Alan & Gill Bridgewater

Sterling Publishing Co., Inc. New York

"Of all man's works of art, a cathedral is greatest.
A vast and majestic tree is greater than that."

Henry Ward Beecher

Acknowledgments

We would like to thank all the people and companies who have helped us with tools and materials:

Gregg Blomberg, Kestrel Tools, Lopez, Washington, United States (the crooked knife)

Jim Brewer, Freud, High Point, North Carolina, United States (Forstner drill bits)

Frank Cootz, Ryobi America Corp., Anderson, South Carolina, United States (thickness planer)

Nick Davidson, Craft Supplies Ltd. UK, Buxton, Derbyshire, England (wood)

Tim Effrem, Wood Carvers Supply, Englewood, Florida, United States (woodcarving tools)

Dawn Fretz, De-Sta-Co, Troy, Michigan, United States (clamps)

John P. Jodkin, Delta International Machinery Corp., Pittsburgh, Pennsylvania, United States (band saw)

Paragon Communications, Evo-Stick, Stafford, England (PVA adhesive)

Library of Congress Cataloging-in-Publication Data

Bridgewater, Alan.
    Woodcarving basics / Alan & Gill Bridgewater.
        p.   cm.
    Includes index.
    ISBN 0-8069-1334-7
        1. Wood-carving—Amateurs' manuals.   I. Bridgewater, Gill.
    II. Title.
    TT199.7.B7623   1996
    730'.028—dc20   95-44153
                                                                          CIP

    Edited and designed by Rodman Pilgrim Neumann

3 5 7 9 10 8 6 4 2

Published by Sterling Publishing Company, Inc.
387 Park Avenue South, New York, N.Y. 10016
© 1996 by Alan & Gill Bridgewater
Distributed in Canada by Sterling Publishing
% Canadian Manda Group, One Atlantic Avenue, Suite 105
Toronto, Ontario, Canada M6K 3E7
Distributed in Great Britain and Europe by Cassell PLC
Wellington House, 125 Strand, London WC2R 0BB, England
Distributed in Australia by Capricorn Link (Australia) Pty Ltd.
P.O. Box 6651, Baulkham Hills, Business Centre, NSW 2153, Australia
Manufactured in the United States of America
All rights reserved

Sterling ISBN 0-8069-1134-7

Contents

INTRODUCTION

Our intention is to demonstrate in depth the fundamental skills involved in traditional woodcarving, including proper tool use and safety as well as the techniques and first-to-last sequence of cuts necessary to execute a design. *Woodcarving Basics* is both a richly illustrated reference on the craft and an easy-to-use instruction manual complete with a glossary of woodcarving terms.

Aware that woodcarving skills develop from a hands-on knowledge of the shape and function of the tools as well as wood types and their characteristics, we are careful to lead the beginner gently into the craft by what we consider is the most logical and thorough route. We start by taking a look at the tools—what they look like, what they do, how to use them safely, and how to keep them in good order. We present a guide to wood types and their characteristics—what the wood looks like, how it performs and finishes, along with our thoughts about wood usage and conservation.

Then we gradually expand the craft of woodcarving by, as it were, showing you how to cut deeper and deeper into the wood. We follow through the craft in much the same developmental way as the craft must have evolved. That is, we start by explaining how to use archetypal tools like the knife, axe, and adze to whittle, incise, and chip carve, and then we go on to explain how to use more sophisticated chisels and gouges to make more complex marks.

Just as an apprentice would have traditionally started out by being shown how to cut shallow marks with a knife, and then gradually introduced to more complex mallet and gouge carving, so you the reader will gradually work through the book from simple knife and adze work to sophisticated relief work and sculptural carving.

In the midst of the sections on technique, there are exercises that are designed to lead the beginner through a workout of very specific skills. Once you have mastered the fundamentals, you will be able to try your hand at one or all of the projects in the final section.

If you think of this book as being the most complete, the most in-depth foundation course in woodcarving that you are ever likely to take, then you won't go far wrong!

Alan and Gillian Bridgewater

Chapter 1

TOOLS, SAFETY, AND SHARPENING

There are literally hundreds of tools that a woodcarver might well use at some stage—everything from knives and gouges to drawknives, saws, and drills. That said, when we started woodcarving, we only needed a tenon saw, a coping saw, a mallet, a couple of secondhand gouges, and a couple of knives. And then again, we know a full-time professional woodcarver who specializes in bowls, working with no more than an axe, an adze, and a selection of knives.

Your tool requirements will depend directly on just what you have in mind to carve. We recommend that you look through this section on tools, read about how to care for the tools, study the projects and the chapters on techniques, and then make decisions in light of your needs and ambitions.

Safety

The first priority of any woodcarver should be to avoid accidents. Every cutting situation, whether with hand tools or power tools, should be approached with the intention of following a consistent set of safety techniques.

Safety Checklist—Mental and Physical Acuity ✓

- Never work while tired or taking medication. Whenever you are tired, stop or take a break. Accidents are most likely to happen when you are tired. Medication and alcohol can affect your perception and reaction time.
- Try not to rush the job. Trying to finish a step in a hurry leads to errors and accidents. The stress of rushing the job also leads to early fatigue.
- Be aware of your attention, or lack of it, to the job. Daydreaming or thinking about another job while operating a power tool or handling a sharp hand tool can lead to accidents. Repetitive cuts lend themselves to daydreaming, so be doubly careful when making them.
- Avoid distractions. Conversing with others, unfamiliar noises, and doors opening and closing are all distractions in the workshop. Never surprise someone who is working with tools.

Safety Checklist—Clothing and Protective Gear ✓

- Dress properly for your own physical protection. Clothes should be loose enough to permit easy bending but not loose enough to get caught in moving tools.
- Remove all rings, bracelets, necklaces, etc., that may become caught. Keep your hair, cuffs, jewelry tied back and out of harm's way.
- Protect youself. Always wear protective glasses or goggles. If the area is noisy, wear ear plugs or muffs to preserve your hearing and minimize fatigue. Wear a dust mask to protect against sawdust and microscopic particles. Some wood dusts are toxic, and all are not good to breathe.

Beginners, regardless of their age, should learn to respect and care for their tools as a condition of learning how to use them.

A basic safety checklist should start with assessing your mental and physical acuity. Are you able to concentrate and work safely?

Another key element in ensuring safety is the condition of your general working environment. Follow a set list of procedures for keeping a safe work area that includes attention to general housekeeping.

Safety Checklist—General Working Environment

- Keep your workshop neat and clean. A dirty or cluttered work area provides tripping hazards. Excess dust can become a breathing hazard. It is also more pleasant to work in a clean, organized work area, as well as safer.
- Make sure your work surface is at a comfortable height with plenty of room to set out your tools and workpiece.
- Evaluate the lighting conditions in your workshop. Adequate lighting is necessary to the safe use of sharp hand tools or the operation of power tools. Shadows and dim lighting increase fatigue and contribute to measurement errors.
- Make sure that a grounded outlet of correct amperage for your power tools is close by. This outlet should be below the level of your work table so that any electrical power cords will not interfere with work. Keep all electrical cords and extension cords free of entanglement with loose materials. Be certain all power cords are not worn or damaged but in good repair.
- Keep the floor area clear and wipe up all spilled liquids immediately to prevent a slipping hazard.
- Look over your wood stock, inspecting for loose knots, twists, cupping, or wet lumber. These conditions can cause trouble, especially with power tools.

Your safety checklist should include making sure that you are wearing appropriate clothing that is comfortable but not too loose, as well as approved eye protection such as goggles or safety glasses and a dust mask when needed.

You should follow a consistent set of general safety rules when using sharp hand tools or power tools. Always read and study the owner's manual

Safety Checklist—General Power Tool Safety Rules

- Read and study the owner's manual. This will familiarize you with the mechanical features, their adjustments, and general instructions for operating the tool. If you are uncertain, seek help and advice.
- Use whatever safety-related devices are provided by the manufacturer, such as guards and hold-downs.
- Only use a tool if it is in good condition.
- Be certain the switch operates properly.
- Never allow someone else to turn on a power tool for you.
- Do not leave any machine unattended with the power on.
- Be aware of the potential danger in certain situations when operating power tools. Keep your hands on top of the workpiece. Hold the workpiece down fair and square on the work table.
- Make sure the power tool is properly grounded with an appropriate three-prong electrical plug and grounded receptacle that is equipped with a ground fault interrupter (GFI).
- Lock master switches or power sources to keep idle tools from being used by unauthorized individuals.
- Never leave children alone in the workshop.
- Do not use any tools while under the influence of medication, alcohol, or when fatigued.
- Keep your tools in good order, and keep your work area organized and clean.

for the specific tool, and use whatever guards or safety-related devices such as hold-downs that are provided by the manufacturer.

Most important for maintaining a safe workshop is to develop a consistent and logical strategy for approaching your work. The safety checklists are part of a total approach to safety and efficient work practices. Each of the checklists should be used together with the others to comprise a complete basic list of considerations. In addition to this basic list of safety points, you should practice each new technique with safety foremost in your mind, asking yourself: What is the best way to proceed? Always think through what you plan to do as far ahead as you can, so that you can find alternative approaches and eliminate potential problems before they happen.

Safety with an Axe

The level of success and safety when using an axe depend to a great extent on the way you stand and on your concentration. As the axe is potentially a very dangerous tool, it needs to be used with care and caution. It's not a tool to use when you are tired or likely to be distracted. Unlike, say, the thrust of a gouge—which can be controlled or pulled back—once an axe has been swung, then there's no pulling back—the weight and fast momentum of the swinging head are going to follow through.

In use, if you stand in a strong, stable, well-balanced, feet-astride position—with a chopping block at the correct height—then you won't have problems. It's a good idea, once you have an axe, to get yourself several large, knotty, tree-section blocks, all about 18in (46cm) in diameter but at different heights. Make sure that the blocks are secure, free from wobble and movement, and then, at least, you can always work at a safe, comfortable height. The workpiece needs to be well supported with one hand, while the axe is held and swung with the other. See the technique and project sections for hands-on guidance.

Safety Checklist—General Hand Tool Safety Rules

- Think through each operation before you execute it. Use an alternate technique if the one you plan will put you at risk of an accident.
- Only use a tool if it is in good condition. Keep your tools sharp.
- As always, wear protective equipment such as safety glasses or goggles and dust masks.
- Always keep you hands and limbs well clear of the cutting part of any tool.
- Never let children "play" with tools while you are working. Never leave children alone in the workshop.
- Do not use any tools while under the influence of medication, alcohol, or when fatigued.
- Keep your tools in good order, and keep your work area organized and clean.

Choosing and Using Tools

Axe

We all know what an axe looks like—it needs no introduction. As to which came first—meaning the axe or the adze—it's not so easy to say. Perhaps we can only note that, in overall shape, structure, and size, the carver's axe and adze are close cousins.

In historical terms, it was the axe that served as the woodcarver's primary tool. Long before there were sawmills, and planes, and gouges, and all the other woodworking tools, the woodcarver used the axe to do just about everything from felling trees and cutting logs into timber to roughing out, making bowls and troughs, and, of course, for doing all the general workaday hewing and shaping.

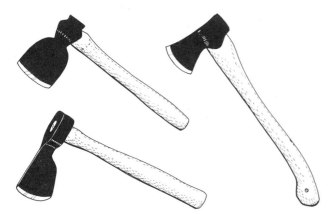

1–1   Many small axes and hatchets are widely available—all of a slightly different shape, size, and function. We can vouch for the following: (top left) the English "Kent" hatchet—quite heavy with a generous head; (bottom left) an American hatchet with a 2⅝in (67mm) cutting edge—the notch on the underside of the head makes this a good tool for controlled hewing and shaping; (right) a Swedish axe with a good head shape and a very comfortable handle. The shaped butt at the end of the handle means that you can let the tool slide through your hand without fear of losing your grip.

In the context of modern American and European woodcarving by both professionals and hobbyists, as well as in the context of contemporary folk, ethnic, and tribal woodcarving from around the world, the axe is still the best tool for the swift and accurate removal of large amounts of wood.

Questions on Axes

Question   Is an expensive handmade Swedish axe really any better than an inexpensive mass-produced axe?

Answer   In almost all instances a handmade tool is a better-quality tool than one stamped out on a machine. This has nothing to do with elitist fads, but rather it is a statement of fact that relates to the physical properties of the steel. A laminated steel blade is easier to sharpen and will stay sharper longer than a mass-produced blade of uniform solid steel.

As to the best type of axe, that depends on what it is you have in mind to carve. For example, if you want to carve a large trough, then you probably need a broad-bladed hewing axe for roughing out the log and for splitting, and a smaller, lighter axe for shaping.

When you decide that you need a short-handled hewing axe, then the specific shape will depend on the source country. Hewing axes made in England, Sweden, Germany, Italy, the United States, or wherever all differ in shape, with the curve of the handle and the profile of the head harking back to various traditions and ways of working from particular regions.

From our experience, we favor two axe types: the Swedish short-handled broad axe with a 10½in (26.7cm) cutting edge that we use for heavy hewing and roughing out, and a small-headed American hatchet with a lightweight blade about 4in (10.2cm) long that we use for fine-shaping (see **1–1**).

Question   Is it okay to use an axe that has a turned, round-section handle?

Answer   Not only does the turning procedure weaken the grain structure of a length of wood—and this alone makes a turned axe handle a bad idea—but, even worse, a round-section handle is difficult to grip and hold. A shaped handle on the other hand—one with an egg-shaped cross section and a flared butt—makes for a more comfortable and a safer grip.

Question   What is the best axe head shape?

Answer   There are at least 25 different head shapes and sizes available in just the stack of catalogs and books we have. And without doubt, the size and weight of the head alone are significant factors to consider depending on your build and body size. Our best advice is to wait on buying an axe until you have a specific need. It is this need that will, to a great extent, answer the question.

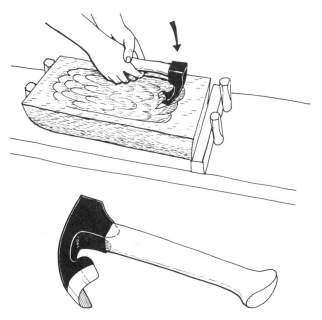

1–2 A short-handled gouge adze of this character is particularly good for carving hollows in bowls and dishes. The shape of the head and the shape of the handle butt both go to make a tool that is easy and comfortable to use. In use—with the workpiece held secure—the tool is swung with a two-handed wrist-pivoting action.

1–3 The large adze is a great tool for carving the shallow curves in slab-wood chair seats. With the workpiece being held firm, the tool is swung in a slow, easy movement—like a pendulum. If the blade is sharp, and the seat slab is slightly green, and you are only aiming to remove skims of waste, then the momentum carries the blade through as easy as, well, cutting through cheese!

Adze

The adze is an axe-like hand tool that has a blade set at right angles to a wooden handle or shaft. In use, the adze is swung in an arch—in much the same way as an axe—and used to remove scoops of wood (see **1–2**).

Adzes range in size from small examples that can easily be held and swung in one hand to massive specimens that needs to be held in both hands with arms outstretched and swung like a pendulum (see **1–3**).

If you are unfamiliar with the adze, and can't quite see how it can be used in a woodcarving context, then best think of it as being more akin to a chisel or gouge blade set at right angles to the handle. As to whether or not you personally need an adze, it really depends on your carving ambitions. If, for example, you have in mind to carve large bowls, or, perhaps, chairs and/or stools with slightly hollowed slab-wood seats, then an adze is an amazingly efficient and easy-to-use tool.

The adze—big or small—is primarily a tool that is used when you want to remove relatively large amounts of wood with the minimum of effort. There are several basic pattens of hand adze. We use a deep U-section type known as a bowl-maker's adze. Our particular tool has a 1¾in (4.4cm) wide 6in (15cm) long gouge head, with a flat face, or poll, on the back of the adze head that can be used as a hammer or mallet. Its beautifully shaped 9in (23cm) long hickory handle and deep gouge blade make it the ideal tool for reaching and scooping out bowl and trough hollows (refer to **1–2**). And then again, we have a large old adze that has a shallow gouge-like blade that we use for cutting stool seats (refer to **1–3**). Just like the axe, there are many types and shapes of adze.

In use, the adze is held and swung in much the same way as the axe, with the workpiece being held and supported on a chopping block. That said, whereas you would, in many instances, follow through with the axe and finish up with the cutting edge running into the chopping block, the adze stroke is pulled—or you might say broken—so that the swing becomes more of a scooping or hooking action.

Good advice, if you are a beginner, is to wait on buying an adze until you have a clear understanding of what it is you want to carve, and then buy the shape, size, and type of adze that best suits your needs.

Questions on Adzes

Question How do I sharpen an adze?

Answer An adze is sharpened in much the same way as a gouge. That is to say, it is ground to shape on the grindstone, honed on the oil-stone, and so on. The only difference is that the adze bevel tends to be much longer on the outside of the blade.

Question I see that there are two types of adze blade—one like a chisel and the other like a gouge. Which one is best?

Answer We prefer using the gouge adze, because we find that the corners of the chisel adze tend to dig in and score the wood.

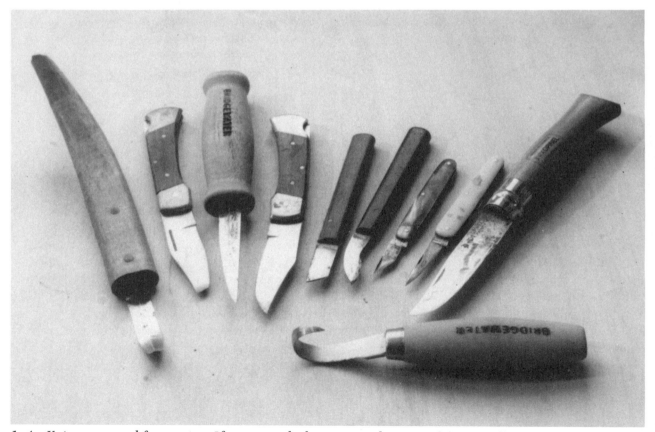

1–4 Knives are good for carving. If you get to be keen on woodcarving, then you will soon start collecting knives. A fearsome array maybe—but each knife gets to be used for a slightly different task. And the good thing is that you can easily shape the blades to suit your own needs.

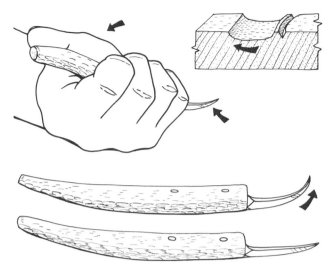

1–5 The Northwest Coast Indian knife—made by Gregg Blomberg of Kestrel Tools—is a very special tool. It takes a bit of getting used to, and the blade isn't easy to sharpen, but it is a very efficient knife. With the thumb pushing hard on the end of the handle, and the blade hooking towards you with a tight scooping action, this knife is good for cutting small hollows. If you enjoy whittling small domestic items, then this is the tool for you. There are several blade curves to choose from.

Knives

After the axe and adze, the knife is one of the woodcarver's primary tools (see **1–4**). From the beginner's viewpoint, the knife has the advantage that is a familiar tool—we all know how to hold and handle a knife. Or do we?

In much the same way as we have slowly built up our collection of gouges to suit our individual needs, so we have searched out our knives. For example, we have a beautiful crooked Indian knife from the northwest coast of North America that we use for carving bowls and masks, we have a Swedish Mora or sloyd knife that we use for whittling spoons and for incising, we have a Swedish hooked knife that we use for dishing out the inside of spoons and for small bowls, we have a French clasp knife for general whittling, we have two Henry Taylor chip carving knives, we have two beautiful old bone-handled penknives that we use for modelling and detailing, we have a couple of really horrible Chinese knives that we have

ground to shape so that we can use them for generally rough work, we have a couple of drawknives that we use for shaping chair legs and poles, and so the list goes on (refer to **1–4**).

As to what is the best knife, once again, it really depends on what it is that you want to carve. You might think that this is a bit lame on our part, but your choice of knife really does hinge on the size and character of the item that you have in mind to carve, on your strength, on the size of your hand, etc. Nevertheless, there are one or two characteristics that make for a good knife. First and foremost, knives needs to be sharp. In our experience, the sharpest knives tend to be either old and/or knives made from laminated steel.

The length and shape of the handle and blade really depend on the size of your hand and the grip you intend using. For instance, if you want to hold the knife like a dagger for engraving or for scooping out a hollow, then it's good to have a knife with a long handle that tapers up towards the butt and a short blade. In this context, the taper provides good leverage for the thumb. And then again, if you want to hold the knife in a grasping, tight, thumb-braced cut for whittling—similar to holding a knife for paring an apple—then the handle needs to be small so that it fits into your hand. One of my favorite knives—the crooked knife made by Gregg Blomberg of Kestrel Tools—has a handle with a most curious unpromising shape (see **1–5**). In fact, when I first came to use it, I started by cutting my finger! In use, it is clasped dagger-like so that the thumb is pushing with leverage against the end of the handle. By rocking the wrist and pressing the thumb against the handle, it is possible to remove the waste wood with a rapid scooping-and-hooking action.

All this leads to an awareness that there are just about as many knife types, handles, blade shapes, holds, and uses as there are woodcarvers. Our advice to beginners is to keep your eyes open for different knives new and old—and to start a collection.

Questions on Knives

Question I have read that only backwoods carvers use knives—for making whittlings and such. Is this correct?

Answer Although there may be some truth in thinking that folk/ethnic woodcarvers favor knives, we suspect that this has more to do with knives being all that people of limited means could afford. As to whether or not so-called sophisticated carving can be done with a knife, well, of course, the answer is most definitely yes! Knives, gouges, chisels, or whatever, the woodcarver goes for the tool that best does the job.

Question Do I need a drawknife?

Answer With the observation that a drawknife is, in effect, a long knife with a handle at each end, we find that drawknives are best used for carving and shaping large sculptural forms and for shaping greenwood poles and staves. And, of course, if you are going to get yourself a drawknife—a tool that needs to be held and used with both hands—then you also need a "donkey" or shaving horse to hold the workpiece (see **1–6**).

1–6 If you have in mind using a drawknife to shape sticks and poles for furniture, then you need to have the wood held in a vise or clamp. The traditional bench—called variously a "donkey," a shaving horse, a bodgers bench, and one or two other names besides—is designed specifically to be used with the drawknife. In use, the workpiece is pushed between the bearing surface and the crossbar, and then held in place by the pushing action of the feet. With all the heights and levels being fully adjustable, the whole operation makes for a very comfortable and efficient way of working.

Chisels, Gouges, and Mallets

There are so many beautiful woodcarving chisels and gouges on the market—we estimate that there are at least a thousand—that it is all the more confusing for the beginner to make a choice.

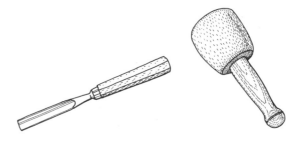

We find that for the general run-of-the-mill, day-to-day tasks we use around twenty tools. Okay, so we do have a workshop full of gouges, and they do all occasionally get used, but most of our carving is done with a handful of carefully selected gouges and chisels. By "selected," we really mean that each and every tool has been carefully chosen in the light of such and such a problem that couldn't be managed with our existing range of tools.

The problem is—and you will find this out for yourself when you start carving—that sooner or later, you will come across a tricky detail, or a piece of undercut modelling, or an extra large carving, or whatever that requires a chisel or gouge of a specific shape, size, and character. It is hard not to become a relentless collector of special-use gouges and chisels.

Certainly the woodcarver's most important tool—the tool that gets used more than any other—is the straight gouge, but it can't do everything. The time will come when you need to use a bent gouge, and then a spoon gouge, and then maybe you will need to use two spoon gouges . . . and so the fun begins.

To make things even more puzzling for beginners, terms and descriptions vary from one manufacturer to another, from one English-speaking country to another, and from one book to another.

Most manufacturers of chisels and gouges, be they English, American, Swiss, German, or whatever, use an age-old coding system known as the Sheffield list. Although at first sight, the code looks to be logical, with, for example, the range of No. 6 straight gouges all having the same characteristic of curved cross section no matter what their width, confusion arises because all the manufacturers add their own prefix code. Some manufacturers have code numbers and/or letters on each side of the list number. By the time you try to sort it all out, you may not have enough energy left for carving, or you will have become a master code breaker!

If you are a beginner and are already confused—and who wouldn't be!—then our definitions and descriptions that follow are just for you. Our advice, when you are ready to buy a gouge, is to start by determining the width of the blade you need. Then choose the depth of the hollow or

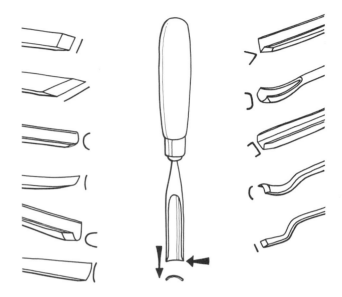

1–7 The cutting shape—the little line or curve the tool makes when the blade is pushed into the wood—is termed the sweep. The best thing to do is to decide on the width and curve of the sweep, then choose the type of tool that suits your needs. If you have doubts, then most good tool specialists will be more than happy to show you the tools close-up.

sweep, and finally decide on the profile of the blade—meaning whether you need a straight, curved, spooned, or fish tail. At this point, you are ready to walk into the store and point a finger (see 1–7 and 1–8).

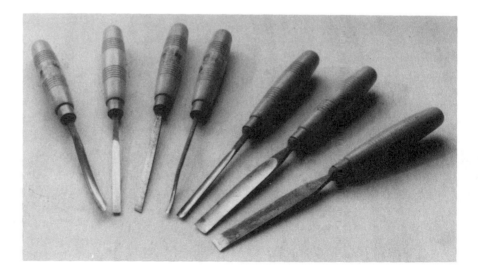

1–8 This set of Henry Taylor tools—English—are really high quality.

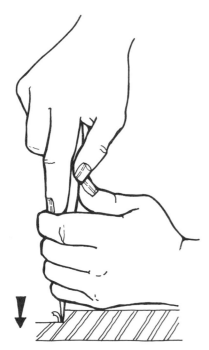

1–9   A straight chisel is one of the woodcarver's primary tools—the tool that is used for most of the heavy setting-in, general workaday tasks.

Questions on Straight Chisels

Question   I have a collection of old woodworking chisels—can I use them for carving?

Answer   If you have a look through woodcarving tool catalogs, you will see that not only do woodcarving chisels have bevels on both sides of the blade, but the total bevel angle is less than on woodworking chisels. You could try a swap with a woodworker who has a set of carving chisels he no longer needs. You can also try regrinding the chisels to suit your own needs.

Question   Why do some woodcarvers grind the corner-sides off their chisels?

Answer   If you grind off corner-sides, then you will more easily be able to slide the blade into difficult-to-reach angles.

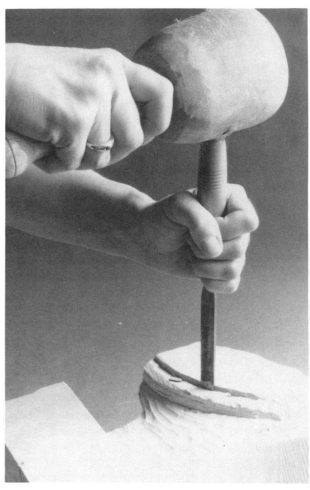

1–10   If you are using a straight chisel for setting-in a stop-cut, then be sure to use a mallet to put a bit of force behind the cut. Don't thump with your fist— your hands are your most valuable tools!

Straight Chisels—Square and Skew

In plain simple terms, a straight chisel is a flat-bladed hand tool that has a cutting edge on one end, a long straight blade, a straight shank between the end of the blade and the start of the handle, and a tang, or spike, that leads off from the shank to run into a wooden handle. If you were to set the cutting edge of a chisel down on the wood, and give it a tap with a mallet, the resultant cut would be unswerving—like a dash. However, the term *straight* relates not to the shape of the cut— all chisels make straight dash cuts—but rather to the fact that the blade along its length is straight.

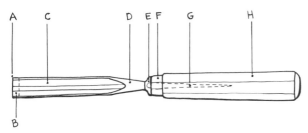

1–11 *Parts of the tool—chisel or gouge: (A) cutting edge, (B) bevel, (C) blade, (D) shank, (E) shoulder, (F) ferrule, (G) tang, (H) handle.*

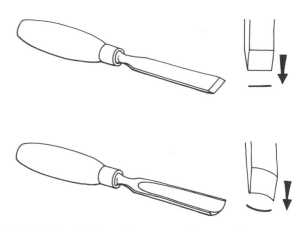

1–12 *If the blade makes a straight cut, then it's a chisel—if the blade makes a curved cut, then it's a gouge; (top) straight chisel, (bottom) straight gouge.*

If you keep in mind that the term straight relates to the shape or profile of the blade along its length and not its cross section, then the rest comes easily. The only difference between a skew and a square straight chisel, is that a skew chisel has the cutting edge set at an angle to the side of the blade.

When you come to buy a straight chisel—square or skew—you will see that they are defined and coded by the width of the cutting edge. So, for example, in one catalog the chisels range in size from ⅟₃₂in (0.75mm) right up to 2in (51mm).

In use, the straight chisel is either held in one hand and pushed with the other (see **1–9**), or held in one hand and banged with the mallet (see **1–10**). The straight blade results in the effort—your push or bang—being targeted directly into the wood being worked.

Straight Gouge

The straight gouge is much the same as a straight chisel—with a cutting edge, a straight blade, a shank and all the rest (see **1–11**); the only difference is that the blade is hollowed in cross section along its length. The hollow is the characteristic that defines the tool as being a gouge rather than a chisel.

If you were to set the cutting edge of a gouge down on the wood and give it a tap, it would produce a curved cut—like an arc, "C," or "U" (see **1–12**). All gouges, to a greater or lesser extent, make a curved cut. The precise shape or curve of the blade is termed the *sweep*. And once again, the term *straight* relates to the shape or profile of the blade along its length.

In use—as with the straight chisel—the straight gouge is either pushed or struck. The straight blade results in a very efficient transferal of energy from the prime mover to the wood.

Questions on Straight Gouges

Question   I have a V-tool—is it a chisel or gouge?

Answer   If a tool makes any other mark than a curved "C" or "U" when the cutting edge is pushed into the wood, then it is properly termed a chisel. After all, if you think about it, a V-tool is no more or less than a "pair" of chisels set at an angle to each other.

Question   Why do some straight gouges have a large bevel on the inside curve of the blade?

Answer   Although most gouges have the main bevel on the outside of the blade with a small inner bevel, many woodcarvers have found that creating a bevel on the inside of the gouge minimizes digging in—meaning when the blade wants to run deeply into the grain. Then again, some carvers grind the corners off their gouges, as mentioned with chisels.

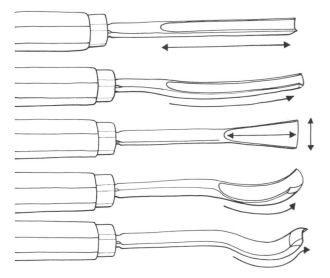

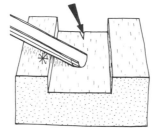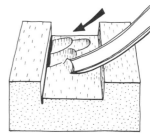

1–14 (Left) As you can see, trying to "waste," or lower, a restricted area of ground with a straight gouge is not such a good idea, because there are "blind" areas that the tool can't reach. (Right) The bent tool, on the other hand—bent, curved, or spoon—is just perfect for scooping into small lowered areas.

1–13 The basic blade shapes—(top to bottom) straight, bent or curved, fish tail, spoon, backbent. Note that the arrows indicate the width of the cutting edge and the useful length of the blade.

Curved or Bent Chisels and Gouges

Once you are clear in your own mind as to the difference between a chisel and a gouge, then the specific attributes of each are simple to define. Having established that the term *straight* does no more than describe the shape or profile of the blade along its length, then it logically follows that the term *curved*—in the context of gouges—also describes the shape of the blade along its length (see **1–13**). A curved tool has a blade that bends or curves from the cutting edge along the length of the blade to the tang. The difficult point for most beginners to grasp is that, for example, the ½in (13mm) No. 6 sweep straight gouge and the ½in No. 15 sweep curved or bent gouge both make the same cut. The difference lies not in the shape of the cutting edge, but rather in the shape of the blade along its length.

As to why you need a bent tool, the answer is beautifully simple: the bend allows you to hook or scoop the blade into dips and hollows that would be inaccessible to a straight tool (see **1–14**).

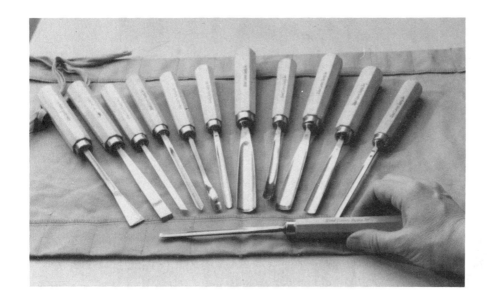

1–15 Using quality tools is pure pleasure—a joy! This particular set comes in the fully honed and polished ready-to-use state.

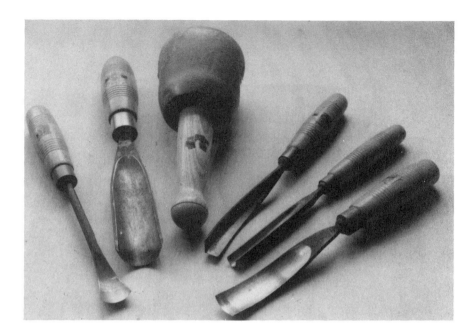

1–16 *These Henry Taylor tools are top-quality English tools—really first class! The only thing that I found was that when they arrived they needed to be honed—and this might be a problem for raw beginners.*

Questions on Curved Tools

Question As a raw beginner, do I really need any bent tools?

Answer As always, it really does depend on what it is that you want to carve. That said, bent tools are especially good for carving in hollows and undercuts as well as inside deep bowls and dishes.

Question I'm keen to start carving—but can't spend very much. Should I settle for getting a couple of expensive brand-new tools or should I get a batch of cheap or secondhand tools?

Answer We would go for the very best quality tools every time. There is nothing quite like the feel of a quality tool (see **1–15** and **1–16**). As for getting secondhand tools, these are often more expensive than new, because typically they are either antique or they are being sold in a market where buyers know well that it takes a lifetime of polishing and honing to get a tool into good condition.

Spoon-Bent Chisels and Gouges

A spoon-bent tool is, as you might now expect, a tool—a chisel or gouge—that has a bent or hooked blade like the shape of a spoon (see **1–17**). A spoon-bent tool is, in effect, a more extreme, tighter curved version of the curved or bent tool as already described. And once again, although a ½in (13mm) wide No. 6 sweep straight gouge, a ½in wide No. 15 sweep curved or bent gouge, and a ½in wide No. 27 sweep spoon gouge all make the same cut, the straight, bent, or spoon shape of the blade along its length means that each tool has been designed for a specific task.

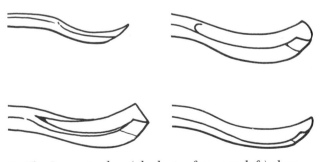

1–17 *Spoon tools—(clockwise from top left) skew spoon gouge, spoon veiner, spoon gouge, and spoon V-section tool. Each one of the cutting-edge profiles comes in a spoon style—it's up to you to choose the shape that best suits your needs.*

Questions on Spoon-bent Tools

Question I can only afford a single spoon-bent gouge; which one should I go for?

Answer Although we can't say for sure, because after all such a lot depends upon the size and character of the carving, we suggest that a ³⁄₁₆in (4.5mm) wide No. 37 is a most useful tool.

Question How do I sharpen a spoon-bent tool?

Answer Spoon-bent tools need to be honed and stropped in much the same way as straight chisels and gouges. That said, as the working part of the tool is so small, you do have to stay away from the grinding wheel.

Questions on Fish-Tail Tools

Question Why bother with fish tails?

Answer With fish tails being longitudinally straight and having a straight shank that widens out progressively to the cutting edge resembling a fish's tail, the benefit of these tools is that the shank isn't in the way when you are trying to carve deep areas. You can see where you are going; the shank doesn't get in the way.

Question What is the difference between a fish tail and an *allonge*?

Answer Although on the face of it, both tools look to be similar in profile—that is, they flare as they get towards the working end—the fish tails are for delicate detail work, while the allonge tools are more suitable for heavy work. Best advice is to get a current catalog and compare shapes, sizes, and usage.

In use, the spoon-bent gouge is used in much the same way as a large spoon. That is to say, the tool is held in both hands—one holding and guiding, the other grasping and pushing—with a digging, levering, scooping action.

Back-Bent Gouge

The back-bent gouge is much the same as the spoon-bent gouge, the only difference being that the blade is bent backwards rather than forward.

Although we personally find that the back-bent gouge has limited use, there are times—on rounded shoulders and on beadings—when it is the best tool for the task.

Fish-Tail Chisels and Gouges

Fish tails, also sometimes called spade tools, can be instantly recognized in that the blade is shaped like the tail of a fish, or you might say like an old-fashioned spade (see **1–18**).

Fish-tail tools—chisels and gouges—are used primarily for tidying up the details and for finishing, with the sharp angle at the side of the tail shape being used when you want to get into undercut areas and tight corners. Their overall shape and structure makes them unsuitable for heavy chopping or roughing out.

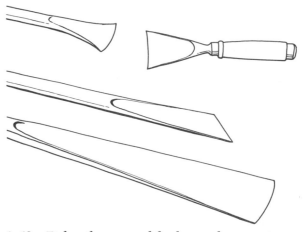

1–18 Fish tails are good for heavy-duty carving and for detail work. The thin shank and the flared cutting edge means that they can be used in restricted areas—most useful when side clearance is limited.

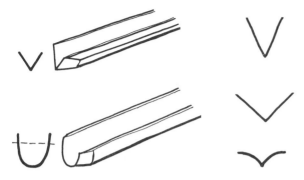

1–19   V-tools and veiners are good for cutting channels and grooves; (left) a V-section tool and a U-section veiner, (right) edge profiles of sharp angle, right angle, and wing.

V-Tools, Parting Tools, and Veiners

The first point to bear in mind is that V-tools and parting tools are in fact different names for the same tool (see **1–19**). V-tools come in three blade profiles—straight, bent or curved, and spoon—and three V-angles. The angles run out at approximately 45, 65, and 90 degrees. That said, there is a special V-tool, called a "wing," that has a very shallow V with curved sides—like the simple shape of a bird in flight.

The veining tool is much the same as the V-tool, the only difference being that instead of being V-shaped in cross section, it is U-shaped.

All the tools—parting, wing, and veiner—are designed to make a "V" or "U" cross section cut. See the techniques section for hands-on advice.

Gouge and Chisel Specials

Apart from the regular range of straight, curved, spoon, and fish-tail chisel and gouge types, there are all manner of specialized tools—meaning tools with strange names, curious shapes, and less-than-obvious usage. For example, some perhaps unenlightened manufacturers sell what they refer to as a "ladies" range. And then again, there are dedicated tools that are designed for a single purpose, like the "Macaroni" that makes a square section trench, and the "Fluteroni" that cuts a trench with slightly rounded corners, and the "dog leg" and "foot" chisels that are used for clearing lowered ground, and so forth.

Handles

As if choosing the shape, type, and size of the chisels and gouges isn't daunting enough, you also have to make decisions about the type of handle. Do you, for example, want a turned handle in a hardwood like mahogany or beech or would you prefer an octagonal-section handle in a light-colored wood like hornbeam? Well, we personally enjoy using both types—it all depends on the task. The feel of a turned handle is wonderful, but, then again, the octagonal section handles do prevent the tools from rolling about. We both like old tools with boxwood and rosewood handles. And, of course, if you want a very specific handle shape, or a plastic handle, or whatever, then most manufacturers are happy to sell you the chisels and gouges without handles (see **1–20**).

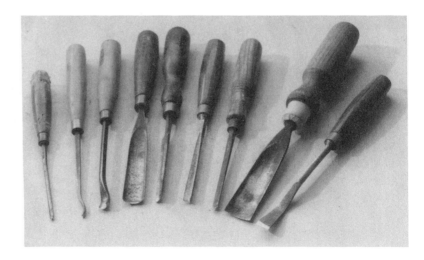

1–20   Handles are a matter of personal choice; (from left to right) a collection of tools bought secondhand—a veiner with a chewed handle that needs sorting out; two spoon tools, both with beautiful boxwood handles; three tools with rosewood handles; an old Henry Taylor V-section tool; a large gouge with a really unpleasant-to-hold homemade handle that needs setting right; and, finally, an old Henry Taylor dog-leg with a rosewood handle.

Question on Handles

Question Turned or octagonal, beech or box—does it really matter?

Answer Surprisingly enough—and we're far from being a pair of stuffy elitists—the shape and feel of a handle does seem to make a difference. For example, plastic handles make our hands sweat, and sharp edge ferrule or overly deep lines around the handle are uncomfortable to hold. Best of all, we like unvarnished boxwood handles, because they feel smooth, warm, dry, and generally good to hold.

Safety—Don't Use Your Hand as a Mallet

Be warned—if you start using your half-closed palm as a sort of a mallet, then you may certainly do damage to the fine bones in your hand. The rule of thumb is—no pun intended—if push gets to bang, then you need to use a mallet. Our advice in the first instance—if you are a beginner—is to choose the most inexpensive mallet that you can get your hands on, perhaps even a billet of wood. Try it out for size and weight, and then buy a better tool of a specific weight, when you have a clear idea of your needs.

Mallets

Having chosen you chisels and gouges, you need to buy a mallet. It is possible to use a billet of wood, or make your own. However, you might be thinking that just about any hammer, mallet, or club at hand will do the job, but this is not so. A mallet is one of those tools that needs to be selected with care. The wrong shape, size, or weight of mallet can result in unnecessary muscle fatigue and misplaced blows.

We currently use three types: a turned wooden mallet with an ash handle and a 3½in (9cm) diameter beech head; a mallet with a rubber-type head; and a mallet with a heavy lump of turned burr wood for a head (see **1–21**). Once again, the mallet types all have different uses. The heavy burr is great for roughing out, the beech mallet is good for everyday work, and the lightweight rubber-head mallet is good for fine details.

1–21 *(Left to right) A mallet made from a heavy turned burr, very heavy and good for huge roughing out; a lightweight Henry Taylor beechwood mallet that gets a lot of use; a very inexpensive rubber mallet that is good for delicate tapping; an adze that gets to be used as a general-purpose mallet-cum-hatchet.*

It's not so easy, though, to say that you should use this or that mallet without knowing your strength and what it is that you want to carve. We say this, because mallets are, more often than not, sold by size and weight. For example, one well-known tool supplier from the United States sells mallets ranging in weight from 12oz (340.2g) through to 30oz (840.5g). Another catalog lists mallets with all manner of round, square, and cylindrical heads.

Bench, Vise, Holdfast and Clamps

Although the woodcarver's bench might be anything from a carefully designed carpenter's bench to an old table, certain requirements are essential. For example, the bench must be four-square and stable with a thick surface, heavy, and strong enough to take a variety of clamps, vises, and holdfasts (see **1–22**).

The size and shape of the bench and your choice of holdfast are governed by your carving ambitions and available space. For example, when we are carving a life-size figurehead, we work on a massive bench that we built with rough-sawn timber and bolts. All we do is heap a pile of old sacks on the bench, set the carving down on the "nest," and then start work. In this instance, the mere weight of the wood ensures that the workpiece stays put.

We find that the how-do-we-hold-the-wood dilemma arises not so much with such large, heavy carvings, but rather with securing smaller pieces. The problem is simply how to hold the workpiece secure—so that we can use a gouge and mallet—while at the same time ensuring that enough of the surface is presented to be worked on. And this is where the strong bench, vises, holdfasts, and clamps come in.

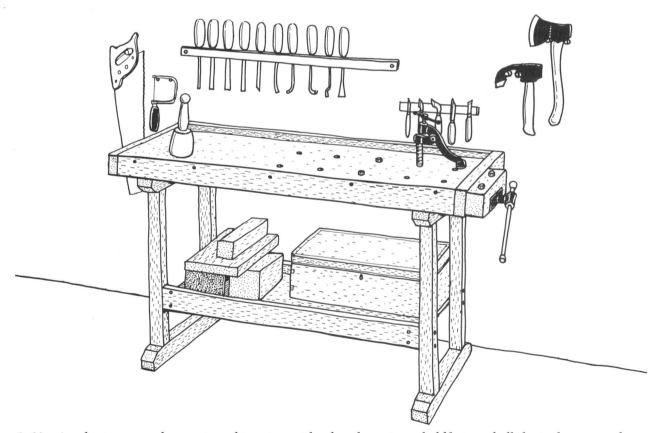

1–22 *Any beginner needs a neat working area with a bench, a vise, a holdfast, and all the tools arranged so that they are comfortably at hand. Most important of all, a woodcarver needs space, plenty of light, and a dry, not-too-warm atmosphere.*

1–23   This Record holdfast is the perfect hold-down for flat work. In use, we usually butt the workpiece up against a bench stop and have the holdfast arranged so that the wood can be moved easily with the least bother. Note the little pad of plywood stuck to the face of the working end—this helps protect the workpiece from being dented.

We usually hold boards and panels flat-down with the holdfast and a couple of wooden stops. We fix the wooden stops as a block to fit the workpiece—like a little wall—butt the workpiece hard up against the stops, and then screw down the holdfast (see **1–23**). The stops prevent the workpiece from sliding across the bench, and the holdfast prevents the piece from bouncing up and down. We occasionally cut and shape the wooden stops so that they also help hold the workpiece flat-down (see **1–24**).

Another easy-to-make device for holding flat panels is an arrangement of blocks and wedges (see **1–25**). We screw four blocks to the bench so that they butt hard up around the workpiece—leaving one side open—and then we grip the workpiece with two wedges.

To hold larger pieces other than panels, such as sculptural carvings, about 24in (61cm) high, we usually start by gripping them in the vise, and then finish up using the holdfast and/or clamps. We sometimes drill a hole up into the base of the carving, fit a bench screw (see **1–26**), and then fix the carving directly to the surface of the bench.

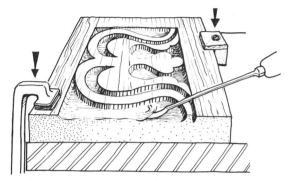

1–24   This is a good arrangement for holding down flatwork—just a screw turn-button and a C-clamp. The thing that I most like about an arrangement of this type is that it's inexpensive and easy to adjust or modify. And of course, if your means are limited, you can leave out the clamp and make a few more screw-buttons.

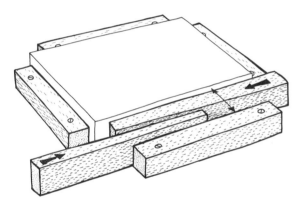

1–25   If you are planning to relief-carve a flat slab, and you know that it's going to take time, then a semi-permanent arrangement of blocks and wedges makes a very satisfactory clamping jig. And, of course, it's easy to see that the position of the blocks can be changed to suit slabs of a different size. Note: We have a whole bunch of long, slender wedges—they are useful for all sorts of clamping, lifting, splitting, and general holding tasks.

As you can see, everything comes back to the need for the bench to be solid and adaptable, and it shouldn't be a big deal if you want to drill a hole through the bench, bang in a few nails, or try your gouge out on the surface. Our best advice, if you are a beginner, is start off with the biggest, strongest bench, stand, or table that you can afford, set it up with a good-quality large-jaw vise, and then take it from there.

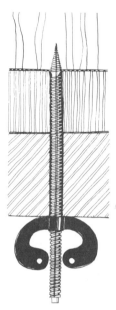

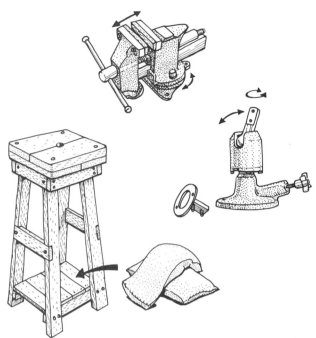

1–26 *The bench screw is just the thing if you plan to make small sculptures. In use, a block of waste wood or ply is glued to the base of the workpiece, a hole is drilled up through the attached block, and then the whole work is screwed to the bench surface by means of the large butterfly nut.*

1–27 *(Left) A homemade bench for small sculptural works needs to be at the right height with a top about 20in (51cm) square. A good estimate for an appropriate height is to have the surface at about the level of your elbow. This particular bench is put together from salvaged timber and bolts. Note that there are holes for a holdfast and bench screw. The platform allows the whole thing to be weighted down with bags of sand. (Top) A large engineer's vise is a handy piece of equipment that can easily be purchased secondhand. (Middle right) There are several multipurpose swivel-type vises on the market—this one has an easily adjustable ball-and-socket head that allows you to reposition the workpiece with the minimum of fuss and effort.*

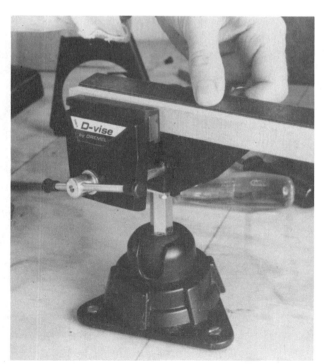

1–28 *This particular vise is just great for small-scale carving. The ball-and-socket movement allows the workpiece to be easily maneuvered.*

Question on Benches

Question The space I have available and my resources are both short—how can I ever manage to acquire a massive bench and vise?

Answer What you need is a small, easy-to-make, stool-like bench—with a bag of sand to hold it stable. You could fit it out with, perhaps, a large multifunction engineer's vise (see **1–27**), or a small model maker's vise (see **1–28**).

Band Saw

The band saw is a power-operated bench tool consisting of an endless metal saw blade running over and driven by wheels. The band saw is a good tool for converting logs into timber and for cutting out blanks in readiness for carving. This is a good tool, if you plan to make a lot of small carved items such as bowls or miniatures, or if you want to make large sculptural carvings from a number of laminated sections.

The band saw needs to be set squarely on a stand or table in such a way that you can feed the wood directly across the cutting surface so that it runs in at the front and out at the back. Having said that, if your workbench is set hard up against the wall, then the length of cut will be restricted by the workpiece running through the machine and butting into the wall. It's best, if you have the space, to have the machine set up on an island or peninsular workbench so that you are able to move freely around the working area.

Before you buy a band saw, you need to be clear in your own mind about the maximum thickness of wood that you are likely to cut. Who, for example, needs a huge machine taking up workshop space, if all you want to carve is thin panels? We personally have a Delta band saw that is well able to cut wood up to 4in (10.2cm) thick (see **1–29**).

1–29   The band saw is useful for cutting out blanks and for clearing the bulk of waste. In use, the workpiece is fed in so far, and then pulled through.

Safety with the Band Saw

In use, the wood is fed into the blade at a steady rate and carefully turned and maneuvered so that the blade is always presented in line with the next cut. However, you must be careful to keep in mind that the band saw is one of the most dangerous power tools that you are likely to use. We say this because, although the cutting action looks to be effortless—with the wood passing through the blade at a gentle almost hypnotic speed—and while the rate of revolution of the blade looks to be low and harmless, you mustn't be deceived into thinking that the machine is a friendly "kitten." **Be warned**, the band saw is notorious for nipping off fingers!

It is simple to use the band saw safely if the workpiece is long—all you do is push it so far in with one hand until your fingers are no less than 6in (15cm) from the blade, and then hook your arm around the machine and pull the workpiece through. If you must cut a small piece—less than about 6in long—then the best procedure is to control the wood with a couple of notch-ended push sticks (see **1–30**).

All in all, if you plan to do a lot of woodcarving, and if you can be vigilant about safety, demanding of yourself to be careful and attentive, then the band saw is a beautifully efficient tool. We recommend that you consult STERLING PUBLISHING COMPANY's *Band Saw Basics*, part of this *Basics* series.

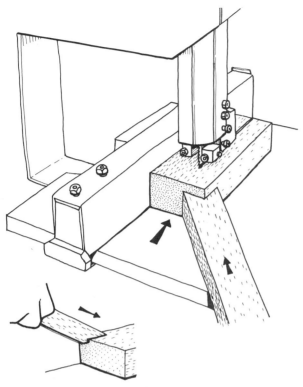

Question on Band Saws

Question I'm a raw beginner—do I need a band saw?

Answer A band saw is a wonderful machine—a great time and money saver. A band saw is good for cutting log wood into timber, for cutting large curves, for swiftly rendering salvaged building timbers into useful sizes, and so on. It is certainly possible to do all this with a hand bow saw, or maybe even with a straight saw and a large-size coping saw, but a band saw does this hard work faster and lets you get on with the more rewarding carving.

1–30 Using the band saw. With regard to safety, the band saw doesn't allow second chances. This being so, if the workpiece is small, then push it just so far with a bird's-mouth push stick, and then pull it the rest of the way through. If you don't like using push sticks, then try a couple of spikes—like ice picks.

Scroll Saw

The scroll saw—sometimes called a fret saw—is the perfect machine for sawing relatively thin sections of wood—meaning wood as thin as veneer and up to planks 1¾in (44mm) thick. With a flat work table and a fine-toothed saw blade that jigs up and down, a scroll saw is wonderfully easy to use. Our particular machine shown in **1–31** is well able to cut out all manner of small sections ranging from panels for relief carving to blanks for spoons.

1–31 A scroll saw is the perfect piece of equipment for carvers who enjoy working on a small scale, or carvers who get to use a lot of thin sections of wood such as furniture makers. This particular machine not only takes coping saw blades as well as fretsaw blades, but better yet, the blades can be fitted so that the teeth face towards the front or towards the side.

1–32 Although the up-and-down action of the scroll saw blade is relatively safe, it does mean that the workpiece needs to be held down hard on the cutting table. Beginners take note: the teeth must always be pointing down.

Safety with the Scroll Saw

A scroll saw is the perfect machine for nervous beginners and even for children with adult supervision.

In use the scroll saw is safe as long as you are familiar with the workings of the machine, you make sure your clothes and hair are tied back out of harm's way, the blade is well adjusted, and the workpiece is fed into the machine at a steady rate (see **1–32**).

If you have had enough of using a hand coping saw, but aren't ready for a band saw, and if you have in mind to concentrate your woodcarving efforts on small section work, then a scroll saw is the answer. We recommend that you consult STERLING PUBLISHING COMPANY'S *Scroll Saw Basics*, part of this *Basics* series.

Handsaws

All woodcarvers need a good selection of handsaws. We have several inexpensive use-until-they-are-worn-out crosscut type saws what we use for all the general day-to-day cutting and roughing, a bow saw with a throwaway blade that we use for sawing wet log wood, and a coping saw that we use for small work and for piercing holes in thin sections of wood.

Abrasive Tools

Although we personally like to see as much texture as possible—a tooled finish, meaning all the marks left by the gouges—and although we try to avoid using dust-making tools, there are times when woodcarvers need to sculpt a surface round or rub a surface smooth. This is where the abrasive tools come in.

Basically there are four types of abrasive tools. There are the open-toothed shapers, or Surform tools, that are used for forming and trimming (see **1–33**)—a bit like a plane. There are heavy-duty traditional-type rasps and files. There are smaller, variously shaped rasps called rifflers, and there are, of course, the various abrasive papers. There are also now all manner of rotary power abrasive tools. We modestly recommend our book *Power Tool Woodcarving*, also from STERLING PUBLISHING COMPANY. In it, we tell you all that you need to know about these new tools and how to use them.

As to the tricky question of when to use abrasives—tools and/or papers—it depends on your approach. For example, there are minimalist carvers who like every took mark to show, and who would consider the use of abrasives as being in some way or other a slur on the integrity of their craft. On the other hand, there are carvers who desire to remove every last tool mark to leave the surfaces smooth.

Our best advice, if you are a beginner, is, in the first instance, to concentrate your efforts on finding out how to use the cutting tools—the gouge, chisel, adze, and knife—and then only use the abrasive tools to tidy up. We say this because it is all too easy to take a rasp or file and a pack of graded sandpapers and to, as it were, smear all the surfaces down to an overall blurred finish. Don't be mistaken, however; we are not advocating a purist approach with every tool mark being on view. All we are saying is familiarize yourself with the cutting tools before opting for using rasps and such.

If you do decide to go in for a lot of dust-making tools, then be sure to get yourself a dust-removal machine and a mask.

Question on Abrasive Tools

Question I've read about a carver who does everything with a chain saw and a heap of rasps—so why bother with chisels and gouges?

Answer Certainly there are carvers who favor such tools, but if you research the subject, you will find that they generally go in for making huge bowls, large free-form sculptures, or huge smooth abstracted forms, with the emphasis being on large and smooth. For our part, we find that files and rasps leave the wood looking dry, rough, and damaged.

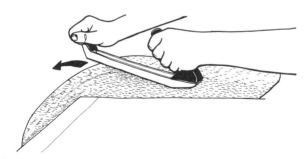

1–33 *If you plan to carve large, smooth sculptural forms, then Surform tools are perfect for skimming a surface down to a smooth scoured finish. For best effect and the most efficient cut, the Surform should be used either with or across the run of the grain.*

1–34 *The drill press is one of those machines that is so efficient that we often take it for granted. We use our machine for clearing the bulk of waste from inside bowls, for lowering ground waste around reliefs, for pieced work, and for all manner of carvings in between.*

Drill Press and Bits

Not counting all the hand tools—the gouges, chisels, etc.—the drill press is one of the most useful pieces of equipment. You might think that a drilling machine is only good for drilling holes, but actually a drill press is a wonderfully versatile labor-saving machine.

We use a drill press for lowering the waste, for hollowing out the difficult-to-reach areas within a complex relief carving, for clearing the waste from bowls, for running small router bits, for roughing out contours and profiles, and so on.

We have a large Delta bench drill press (see **1–34**). It doesn't wobble, move, or make odd noises; it just gets on with its task of boring out holes. For a small workshop, our machine might seem to be overly large and heavy, but its very weight and stability are the positive qualities that make it so useful. If you enjoy carving, and if you want to do more of it faster, and with less sweat and effort, then you will find many uses for a drill press. Our best advice, if you are a beginner, is to start with the basic hand tools, and then purchase a drill press when you feel the need. Experience tells us that a large machine is a better deal in terms of money and capacity than a small machine.

Safety with the Drill Press

In use, the drill bits are fitted in the chuck, the workpiece is clamped securely to the work table (see **1–35**), the power is switched on, and the hole is drilled. It sounds very easy, straightforward, and safe, and it is as long as you follow basic safety rules: Be familiar with the controls, wear goggles to protect your eyes, tie back your hair and clothes, make sure that the guard is down, use a clamp for holes bigger than ½in (13mm), and generally work at the recommended speed. And as with all tools and machines, we must emphasize that you never leave children unattended with the machine.

1–36 *If you want to swiftly clear the waste from flat panels, then Forstner drill bits are the best tool for the task. The cutting action results in a hole with a clean base and smooth sides.*

As to the best drill bits, this really depends on the task. There are many bits to choose from: standard bits, spoon bits, multispur bits, flat bits, spade bits, auger bits, and more. There are even bits that cut out discs and rosettes.

We favor using Forstner drill bits (see **1–36**). We have a large set made by Freud that cope with just about every task that we put before them; they bore straight down through awkward side and end grain, through hard knots, and through just about any wood that we could mention.

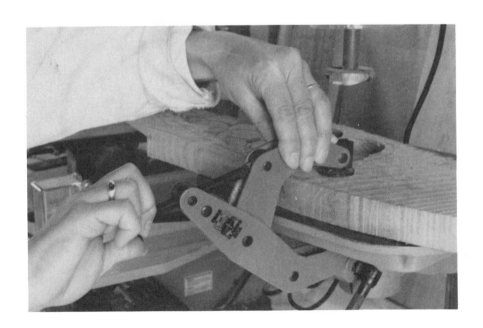

1–35 *If you are going to use a drill bit bigger than ½in (13mm) diameter, then be sure to hold the workpiece secure with one or more clamps.*

Drawing and Measuring Equipment

Woodcarvers need measuring and drawing equipment to make preliminary sketches, to draw plans, to square up the wood, to draw out circles, to step off measurements, to make marks on smooth and rough wood, and so on. Of course, as with all the other tools, your needs will relate directly to your woodcarving intentions. We will describe how we operate, and then you can modify the equipment we use to suit your individual needs.

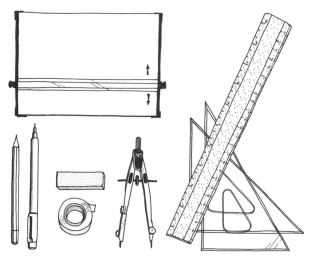

1–37   Drawing equipment. A good starter kit includes: (top left) a drawing board with a parallel motion—a must if you have in mind to design large panels and such; (bottom, left to right) hard and soft pencils, a rubber eraser and masking tape, a large compass with a positive action, a ruler marked in inches and metric, and a couple of set squares.

Developing a Strategy of Work

First and foremost we have a huge drawing board on a stand that we use for drawing the designs out to size (see **1–37**). It has a parallel motion and an easy-wipe surface. We find that the whole process of woodcarving is greatly facilitated when we plan everything out and have, where possible, full-size gridded drawings.

We usually make sketches on a pad, make small maquettes—working models—from Plasticine, and then draw the designs out on paper, make tracings, and, wherever possible, make full-size models and details in Plasticine. We keep the master drawings in the house, and only use the tracings in the workshop. Working in this way, we always have a good, clean record of what it is that we are working on.

Once we have the designs on paper and the models, we move out to the workshop and start cutting the wood to size. So we might use a metal tape measure for long pieces of wood, a set square, a wooden ruler, a large wooden T-square that has a 48in (122cm) capacity, a large pair of dividers, all manner of pencils, a felt-tip pen, etc.

With all the rough-sawn wood sized and cut, and later variously glued up and/or planed, we then either fix the tracings directly to the face of the wood and use a hard pencil to press-transfer the imagery, or we pin the tracing to the wall and use a ruler and a pair of dividers to transfer and step-off the measurements. By dividers, we mean a two-legged instrument with an adjustable screw and legs about 9in (23cm) long (see **1–38**).

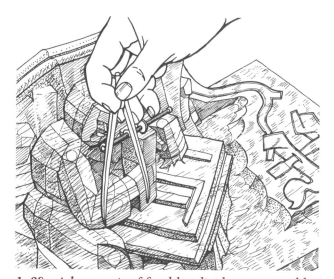

1–38   A large pair of fixed-leg dividers—as used by engineers—is a good tool for checking and transferring measurements from the drawing to the workpiece. We have two pairs: a pair that are so badly made that they hardly hold together, and a pair of really beautiful secondhand dividers that were maybe fifty years old when we bought them. The point is, either buy the best or search around for a good secondhand pair, but don't buy an inferior pair.

In use, we might set the points to the distance shown on the tracing, and then step-off the distance on the wood, and/or we might use the dividers to check the sizes and distances on the carving against those on the drawings.

Having transferred the large bold overall design to the wood, we then use all manner of secondary tools to finalize the details. At various stages along the way we might use hard pencils, masking tape, bits of string and thumbtacks, a small compass, bits of scrap cardboard to make templates, a pair of callipers to check diameters, a knife to make marks, a large wax crayon and/or chalk to shade areas that need to be cut away, and so on.

Having summarized how we go about our work, we must admit that we hadn't realized we used so many tools until we had to write it all down. In light of this realization we can suggest a "starter set" to get yourself going; begin with a small drawing board, a selection of hard and soft pencils, a ream of inexpensive paper from a printers, a pair each of compasses and dividers, and then take it from there.

Sharpening Your Tools

Having said many times that woodcarving is a wonderfully relaxing and absorbing craft, just the thing when you feel stressed up, we ought really to follow this up by adding this proviso—only if you are working with fully honed and stropped razor-sharp tools. There is nothing quite so frustrating as trying to cut a crisp, clean piece of wood with a blunt and/or damaged tool. And just in case you are a beginner and don't yet know, many tools are sold sharpened but not honed. That is to say, the tools are ground to the correct cutting edge, but the actual edge is left relatively thick and unpolished.

All this means that, sooner or later, you will have to bring your tools to good order. Even if you have purchased your knives or gouges in the ready-to-use state, there will come a time when they will need resharpening.

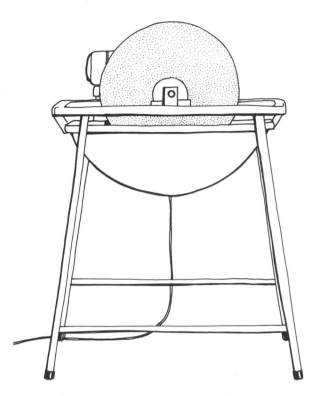

1–39   *If you are a beginner, then a slow-spin water bath grindstone needs to be a priority item. This particular stone is power driven.*

The following list of tools, materials, and sequential procedures will enable you to sharpen even the dullest of tools. For a good general background, we recommend that you consult STERLING PUBLISHING COMPANY'S *Sharpening Basics*, part of this *Basics* series.

Grinding

If your gouge, chisel, axe, adze, or knife is a mess—that is to say, really blunt or maybe with a damaged edge—then you need to start the sharpening sequence by bringing the blade to order on the grindstone.

There are two types of grindstone: there is the motor-driven, high-speed bench grinder with small aluminum oxide wheels that are typically found in mechanic workshops and there is the more traditional, slow-speed hand- or power-driven grindstone with a large-diameter wheel and a water bath (see **1–39**). First and foremost, we must point out that it's very difficult to sharpen a tool on a high-speed stone. A few woodworkers can do it; our son Julian says it's easy, but he's a mechanical engineer. What usually happens is that the shape of the knife edge is damaged and the steel overheats to the extent that it loses its hardness. When you see the blade edge turning blue, you know that this particular area of the blade will no longer be hard enough to work; it needs grinding away and reshaping. All this adds up to the reality that, for our purposes, a small power grinder is not a good idea.

The slow-turning grindstone, on the other hand, is the perfect tool for the woodcarver. As to the rate of spin or rotation of a large power wheel, it doesn't really matter as long as you are aware of the direction it is turning, before you start sharpening. In essence, all you need to know about the spin direction is that if the stone is rotating towards you, then you will, of course, be pushing the tool towards the spin, whereas if the stone is turning away from you, then the tool is, as it were, being dragged away from you.

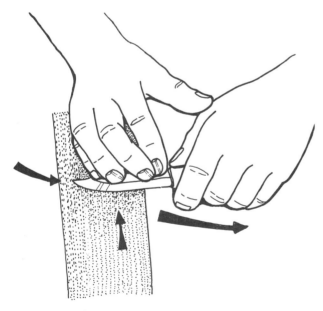

1–40 Grinding a knife. Hold and guide the knife with one hand, press down on the blade with the other, and run the blade across the stone. The bracing action of the linked hands ensures that the bevel and the pressure are constant.

Safety with the Grindstone

Before your grindstone is up and running, make sure you are properly equipped for the task with safety goggles, an apron, and, perhaps, a mask. Once it is spinning, figure out how best to stand and how best to hold and angle the particular tool that you are sharpening. In all instances you need to be standing with your feet slightly apart and your body slightly thrust forward so that your shoulders and arms are braced and in control.

To Sharpen a Knife on the Grindstone   Hold the handle of the knife firmly in one hand, set the blade across the width of the stone so that the back of the blade is in contact and the edge is looking away from your body, set the thumb of your free hand on the hand holding the knife, and press down on the blade with your free fingers (see **1–40**). If you are doing it right, the knife and the two hands will be, as it were, a single braced and controlled whole. With the knife correctly held and braced, tilt the blade so that the edge is in contact, and run the knife in a shallow side-to-side arc to achieve a bevel along the length of the blade. Aim for a shallow angle of about 25 degrees. And, of course, when you have achieved the bevel on one side of the knife, simply turn the knife over, and repeat the procedure.

To Sharpen a Gouge on the Grindstone   Take the gouge in one hand, set the back of the blade on the grindstone, set the fingers of your free hand on top of the gouge—so that the thumb is up towards the handle and the slightly spread fingers are on top of the blade—and then, at one and the same time, lift the handle so that the bevel is in contact with the stone and roll the handle so that the whole bevel comes into contact.

Although the angle at which the bevel of a gouge or chisel needs to be ground is around 15 degrees, what usually happens is that by the time the bevel and edge have been honed, stropped, and generally polished, the actual angle at the cutting edge might be more like 16 or 17 degrees.

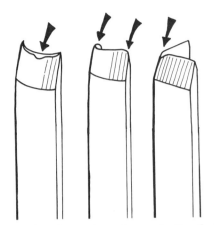

1–41 To judge if a tool needs regrinding hold the blade up to the light and focus in on the profile. (Left) The bevel is faulted, inasmuch as the outer bevel shows as a wavy line. (Middle) Although the rounded shoulders caused by over-rocking of the tool when honing are considered by many to be a fault, lots of carvers do intentionally grind the corners off one or two of the larger gouges so that they can be used for swift roughing out. (Right) If, by chance, you rub away the point of the bevel, then the whole bevel will have to be made good by resharpening.

Questions on Grinding

Question I'm a beginner—do I need a grindstone?

Answer Grinding, actually, is seldom required, since most tools are sold ready to hone. And, of course, when the time comes around that you need to bring a dull or damaged tool to order (see **1–41**), then you could simply use a coarse honing stone. Nevertheless, a grindstone does allow you to customize the shape and bevel of your tools.

Question Can I sharpen an adze or an axe on the grindstone?

Answer Yes, you can. In many ways the procedure can be likened to that of grinding a chisel and gouge. Broadly speaking, the actions are the same, but everything is just done on a bigger scale (see **1–42** and **1–43**).

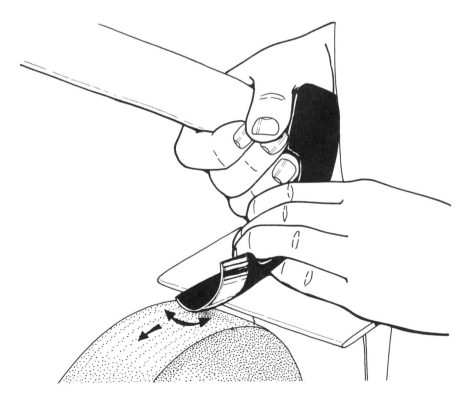

1–42 A bowl adze is ground in much the same way as a large gouge; that is to say, the tool is rolled so that all parts of the bevel come into "equal" contact with the stone. How you hold the head is something you simply work out from adze to adze.

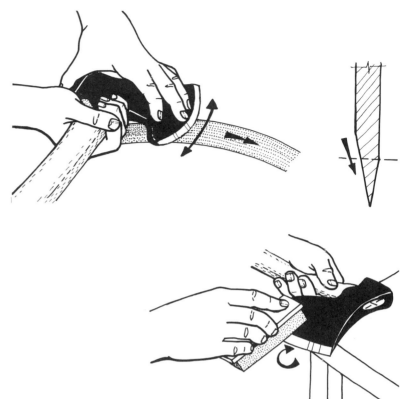

1–43 *Grinding and honing an axe. (Top left) At one and the same time grasp and guide the handle in one hand, press down on the blade with the fingers of the other hand, and run the bevel from side to side across the slow-moving stone. Reverse and repeat the procedure for the other side of the blade. (Top right) Always have the wide bevel looking to your free hand— so, if you are right-handed, have the wide bevel facing left, and if you are left-handed, then have the wide bevel facing right. (Bottom right) To hone, work along the bevel with a small, tight circular motion. Repeat the procedure for the other side of the blade.*

Question How can I grind a hooked knife on the stone?

Answer With difficulty. The problem is how to push down on the blade—see **1–44** for guidance.

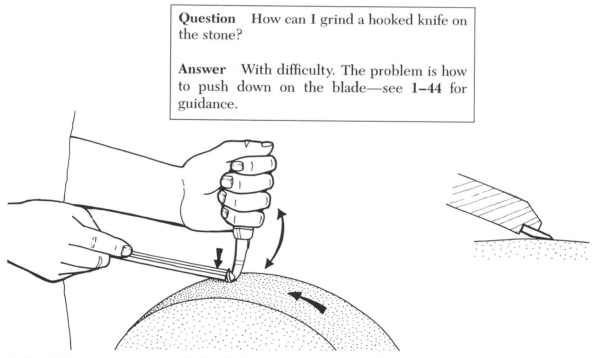

1–44 *When you come to grind a hooked scooping knife to shape, you have to use a bird's-mouth push stick to direct pressure down onto the blade. The working action is: hold and roll the tool with one hand, and push down on the stick with the other.*

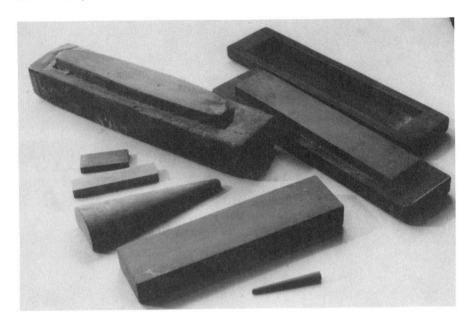

1–45   *You need a collection of honing stones. We have a large stone that is medium on one side and coarse on the other; a medium-fine stone in a lidded box; a very old mis-shapen super-fine stone in a wooden base; a couple of small stones from Sweden; a large slip stone; and a little thin cone slip that we use for small gouges.*

Honing

Once you have ground the bevel to shape—on the knife, axe, adze, chisel, or gouge—then comes the tricky task of honing. Honing can be described as the act of refining and setting the edge of the blade on an oilstone. The modern term *to*

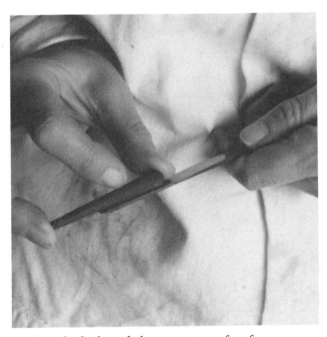

1–46   *The little rod slip stone is perfect for removing the burr from the inside curve of small gouges.*

hone has its roots in the Old English word *han* and the Old Norse word *hein*, both meaning literally "stone." The honing technique involves rubbing the blade with various graded and shaped stones, the object being to remove the pits, scratches, and feathering of waste metal that are left by the grinding procedure. The goal of the honing exercise is to leave the cutting edge clean, polished, and razor sharp.

Although the honing procedure is one of working from rough to smooth through a series of graded stones, this, of course, only applies if your tool is in bad condition. Our usual procedure—the best day-to-day approach—is to stop every ten minutes or so and give the already sharpened tool a few top-up strokes with the smooth stone and the strop. You will find that if you keep your tools well stropped there will be relatively little need for grinding.

There are a considerable number of honing tools on the market—everything from compound diamond grit hones, diamond grit slips, ceramic stones, and aluminum hones to various natural stones with names like Turkey, Charnley Forest, Arkansas, Washita, India, and quite a few others besides (see 1–45). Traditionally woodcarvers use three flat stones in the grades coarse, medium, and fine, and a selection of fine-grade shaped

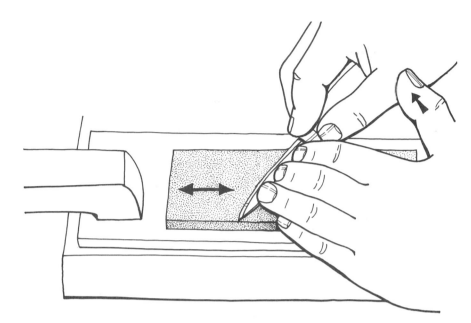

1–47   When the knife is honed, the locked and braced action of the knife and the two hands ensures that the angle of the bevel to the stone is constant.

stones known as slips. The slips are variously shaped so that they match the inside curve of the gouge (see **1–46**). You also need a small amount of light engine oil.

Be mindful that mostly the tools will only need to be set—meaning honed—on the medium- and fine-grade stones. You only need to work through the whole procedure—from grinding, to all grades of oilstone—if the tool has been abused or damaged.

To Hone a Knife   Having fixed the coarse stone flat-down to the bench, dribble a small amount of light engine oil onto the stone, and then set to work. With the handle held in one hand, set the knife down on the stone so that the cutting edge is looking towards your body, angle the back of the blade upwards until the bevel is resting on and in contact with the stone, set the fingers of your free hand down on the top of the blade to increase pressure, and finally move the blade backwards and forward along the length of the stone (see **1–47**).

Having repeated the coarse stone honing on both sides of the blade—until the cutting edge of the bevel is sharper and shinier than when you started—then rerun the procedure on the medium and then the fine stones (see **1–48**).

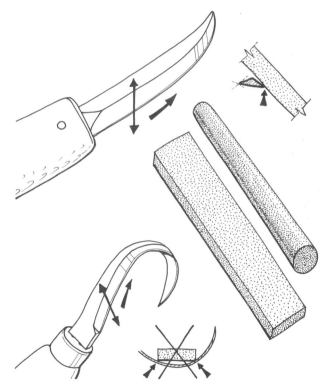

1–48   Hooked and crooked knives are very difficult to hone; all the more so when the bevel is on the inside of the curve—as in the knife at top left—or on the outside of a tight hook—as in the bottom left. We use a small bar stone to stroke the outside bevel on the hook, and use the rod stone for the inside bevel on the crooked knife.

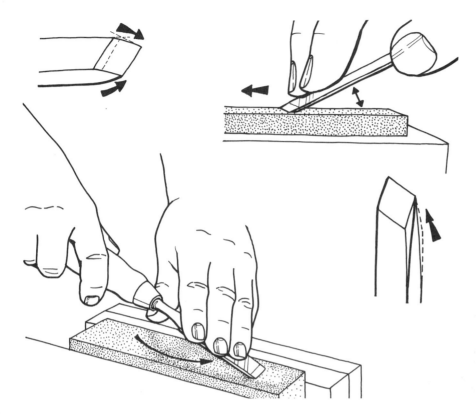

1–49   *Be mindful that both sides of a carving chisel need to be bevelled—with the bevel either flat or rounded. (Top right) Rock the tool to round over the bevel. (Bottom left) Do your best to ensure that both bevels are equal. (Bottom right) Some carvers prefer to grind away the angle on one side of the chisel—the idea being that it enables them to get the chisel into tight corners and angles.*

To Hone a Carving Chisel   Set the coarse stone up as already described, then take the chisel and hold it down on the stone in much the same way as you held the chisel when grinding. Now, with the fingers of your free hand pressing down on the blade, angle the handle up so that the bevel is in contact, and push the tool backwards and forward, nearly the length of the stone (see **1–49**). Do one side and then the other. If all has gone well, there should be an equal bevel and cutting edge on both sides of the blade.

As a beginner, especially watch out for a tendency to slightly lift the tool at the end of the pull stroke, with the resultant effect that the cutting edge rolls and rounds-over, becoming blunt.

To Hone a Gouge   There are at least four different ways to hone a gouge:

First Method   With the tool held in one hand, set the blade down on the stone in much the same way as when you are sharpening a chisel. Set your fingers down on the blade to apply pressure, and then run the blade backwards and forward along the length of the stone, while at the same rolling—or you might say, rocking—the blade so that all parts of the bevel make contact. Continue until the total bevel is equally angled, sharp, and shiny.

Second Method   Repeat the procedure as already described, only this time, instead of running the blade straight backwards and forward along the length of the stone, run it in a figure-eight pattern (see **1–50**). Many woodcarvers claim that not only does the natural flow around the figure eight ensure that all parts of the stone get equal wear, but, better still, they say that the pattern ensures automatically that all parts of the bevel come into contact with the stone.

Third Method   With the tool held at right angles to the stone—or you might say, with the length of the stone running from side-to-side—roll the gouge, while at the same time moving it rapidly from side-to-side.

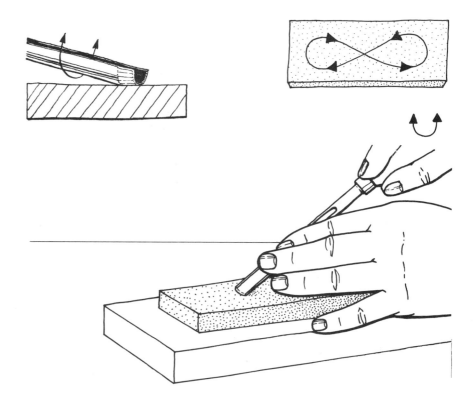

1–50 *Honing a gouge. (Top left and right) Run the tool in a figure-eight pattern along the stone, while at the same time rolling the blade from side to side. (Bottom) Use one hand to guide and the other to rock the blade. The whole procedure is far from easy and needs a lot of practice.*

Fourth Method The method that we prefer is to hold the gouge in the left hand so that the bevel is "looking to the sky"—as if we are about to peer closely at the cutting edge—then take the stone in the right hand and stroke the bevel of the gouge, while at the same time rolling the handle so that the full arc of the bevel comes into contact with the stone (see **1–51**). By being able to see the shape of the bevel up close and in silhouette, and by observing the glint of the cutting edge while working the stone, you can adjust the angle of the stone and/or the tool, and thus sharpen the cutting edge to best effect.

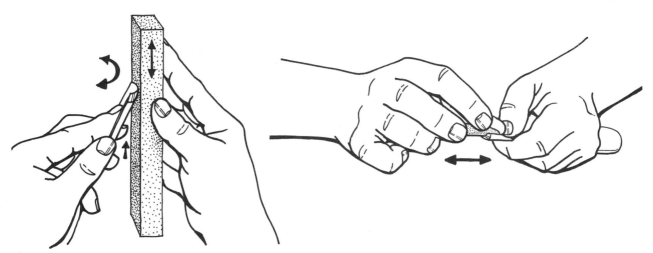

1–51 *(Left) We prefer to move the stone up and down with one hand, and gently rock the tool with the other. (Right) Use the little cylinder/cone slip stone to remove the burr from the inside curve.*

To Hone a Gouge with a Slip Once you have honed the outside bevel of the gouge, then you need to use the shaped slips to bring the inside bevel to order. The procedure is wonderfully simple and direct; all you do is dribble a small amount of oil on the slip, rest the slip inside the curve of the gouge, and stroke the bevel to a polished finish. Bearing in mind that the bevel on the outside of the gouge is at an angle of about 15 degrees, aim to repeat the angle on the very edge of the inside curve, so that the total cutting angle is about 30 degrees (see **1–52**).

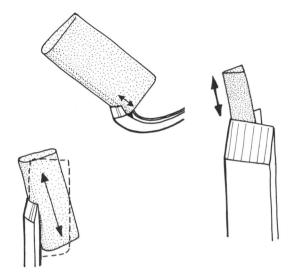

1–52 *Each tool shape calls for a slightly different approach. (Left) The inner bevel needs to be slightly rounded by rocking and rolling the slip. (Middle) If there is limited access, then work with a short joggling action. (Right) Use a V-section slip on the inside angle of the V-tool.*

Questions on Honing

Question Do I need a whole series of graded sharpening stones?

Answer Keeping in mind that the whole sharpening procedure, from the grindstone to the leather strop, is like descending a set of stairs with the top step being rough and the bottom step being smooth, it follows that the more steps you go through, then the sharper the tool. A tool that has only been honed on a rough stone and then stropped cannot be compared, in all fairness, to a tool that has been honed on a series of stones and then polished.

Question Can I hone a drawknife on a stone?

Answer The procedure is much the same as for honing a knife; the only difference is that honing a drawknife is that much easier, because you have two handles to hold (see **1–53**).

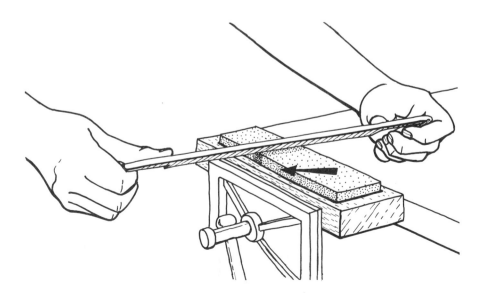

1–53 *Honing a drawknife. Make sliding diagonal passes for the entire length of the blade.*

Question What is the best way to hone a V-section tool?

Answer This is a tricky procedure—see **1–54** for step-by-step guidance.

Stropping

Stropping is the finest and final procedure in the sharpening sequence. The leather strop removes the marks and burrs left by the fine stone. Although there are all manner of leather strops on the market, all we do is drag the blade—of the knife, chisel, gouge, or other tool—across the strop until the cutting edge looks shiny (see **1–55**).

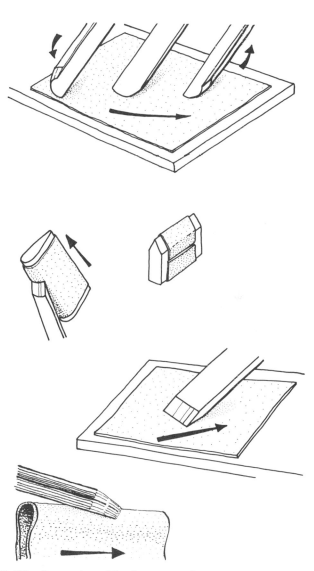

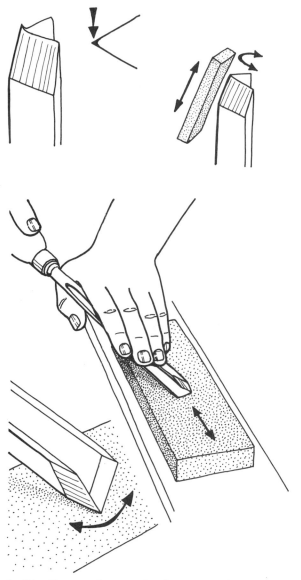

1–54 Honing the V-tool. The action of sharpening will eventually result in a little peaked claw at the point of the V. (Bottom left) To remove the claw, rub the corner on the stone, and then tidy up with the slip. (Top right) Although the cutting edge is in fact slightly rounded, it must look square and clean.

1–55 Stropping. The function of stropping is to remove the wire or burr left by honing. We use various pieces of leather dressed with oil and crocus powder. If you are a beginner and don't quite appreciate the difference a stropping makes, then try to make a few cuts before and after.

Question   Honing and stropping seem to be very time-consuming. Are there any short-cuts?

Answer   We have made a power-driven honing and stropping aid. It consists of a sheet of fine-grade emery cloth mounted on a 9in (23cm) disc of ½in (1.3cm) thick plywood, at the center of which there is a disc of leather, flesh side out, about 6in (15cm) in diameter and an even smaller disc of leather with smooth side out about 4in (10cm) in diameter. The whole works looks a bit like a target. We have it mounted on a faceplate at the end of our lathe, but you could just as well mount it on a slow-speed motor on the bench. In use, we first stroke the blade on the fine emery cloth, and then strop the bevel edge to a high-shine finish on the two inner leather discs. The whole operation is done and finished in seconds.

Chapter 2

WOODCARVER'S WOOD GUIDE

Of all the gifts of nature, trees are part of our lives from first to last. Our first breath, our cradles, our food, shelter and warmth, our books, over half of our medicines, even our coffins are all made possible by trees!

Although trees are all about us, with tens of thousands of different tree types worldwide and with some species still unknown, a great many of us wouldn't know the difference between an oak tree and a sycamore. At the same time, the importance of trees to our economies and standard of living is threatening the loss of vast expanses of this natural resource. Acknowledging the central place of timber in all our lives, we have thought about what it is we as woodcarvers can do to promote the conservation of forests. We have come to the conclusion that knowledge is the key. Our personal thinking is that if woodcarvers find out as much as they can about wood, learn to appreciate its characteristics and qualities, and use this knowledge to be selective, then this will develop respect and encourage conservation.

As a result of our thinking, we only list and describe here the primary timber species that are good to carve and are currently recommended as being suitable alternatives to tropical hardwoods—meaning that we have listed temperate hardwoods and softwoods that come from a sustainable source.

Although we list a range of woods and do our best to describe the general working characteristics of each type, you will no doubt find that your particular chosen workpiece—the bit that you have before you on the bench—differs in almost every detail from our description. Your bit of wood may be a different color, have knots, have a different name, and so on. Part of the joy of woodcarving, part of the adventure and pleasure, is that no block, beam, length, or slab of wood is the same.

Timber Faults and Things You Need to Know

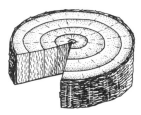

There is no such thing as a perfect piece of wood or a guarantee that your chosen length or block of wood is sound or workable throughout. Certainly the wood might look and smell good, and it might even be described as top quality—and it may even cost you a small fortune—but there is no saying that once the wood is opened—sawn, cut, carved, or drilled—you won't come across a split, or cavity, or a piece of shrapnel, or who knows what!

The best a woodcarver can do is to look out for problem indicators and symptoms at an early stage—best before you have purchased the wood—and then to either go for another piece or try to work around the problems.

Hardwood and Softwood

Hardwood comes from broad-leafed deciduous trees, while softwood comes from evergreens. Hardwood isn't necessarily harder to work or even harder in strength or texture than a softwood. The terms *hard* and *soft* are no more than very general terms that describe the reproductive characteristics of the various trees. So, for example, although balsa is technically a *hardwood*, it is in actual fact one of our softest woods.

Since in woodcarving a softwood is likely to be as workable as a hardwood, then we don't see any compelling reason for listing and/or choosing wood by its *hard* or *soft* designation.

Sapwood and Heartwood

In technical terms, heartwood is the mature wood at the middle of the tree, the wood that forms the heart or spine of the tree, whereas sapwood is the new wood, the wood towards the outside of the tree made up of cells which store the food or nutrients (see **2–1**).

From the woodcarver's viewpoint, sapwood is inferior to heartwood in that it is soft in texture, liable to extreme shrinkage, and subject to disease and insect attack. If you have a choice, go for sound heartwood.

Grain

The term *grain* refers to the arrangement of the fibres that go to make up the wood—the pattern of these fibres that we recognize as being characteristic. So, for example, such and such a wood might be described as being straight-grained, close-grained, coarse-grained, and so on.

Being mindful that the subject of grain is huge—more than enough to fill several books—the following brief descriptions are meant to give you a pointer to set you on your way.

Straight Grain describes a situation where the fibres running along the length of the wood are grouped in straight, parallel bundles. Such a wood tends to be generally user-friendly and easy to carve.

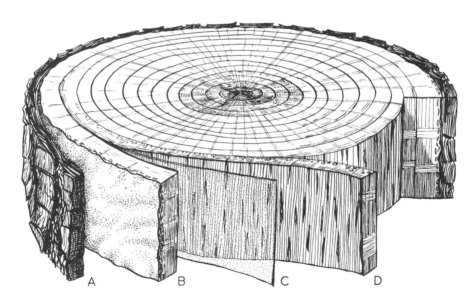

2–1 *The structure of a tree. The slice through the trunk shows: (A) outer bark; (B) phloem—the outer cells of the tree that gradually help to build up the bark layer; (C) cambium—the thin cells that increase the total girth of the tree as they grow; (D) xylem—new wood. Once the cambium cells have developed to the point where they start to divide, the outer portions become the phloem or bark, and the inner ones carry on developing until they become the new wood. As the years pass, with the layers of new wood adding to stem and the total girth, the heartwood becomes inactive and more dense.*

Close Grain   means that the wood was "slow" growing. A slice through the trunk shows that the rings are narrow and packed closely together. Such woods usually carve well.

Coarse Grain   means that the wood was "fast" growing. A slice through the trunk shows wide, loosely packed rings. Such a wood tends to be difficult to carve.

Cross and Diagonal Grain   describes the situation where the fibres of the wood are out of alignment with the run of the piece of timber. Such a piece of wood might well be unpredictable.

Earlywood and Latewood

Latewood, or summerwood, is the dark part of the annual rings, and earlywood is the light-colored rings. It follows that the state and size of the rings are a good indicator of the quality of the wood. Wide rings signal that conditions were good at that growing period; evenly spaced rings are a good sign that the wood is likely to be easy to work; and dark rings suggest that the wood may be difficult to carve. Thus, the woodcarver would do well to find a wood that shows a good number of evenly spaced wide rings with less pronounced dark rings. Or to put it another way, if the dark rings are wide—as is the case with pitch pine— then you can be pretty sure that the woodcarving is going to be tricky.

Blemishes

After the tree has been converted into timber— meaning sawn into boards, planks, and sections— it may happen that the wood changes to an uncharacteristic color, and/or that the wood is actually found to be stained by, say, grease or rust. The wood is then described as having a blemish. Some uncharacteristic stains and colors are desirable— as, for example, the dappled pattern in spalted (see **2–2**) or diseased beech, or the beautiful smoky green color in wych elm—but, for the main part, if a color or feature is out of character and consequently unexpected, then it is considered a blemish.

2–2 Spalting. Spalted wood is no more or less than a form of rot or decay that is caused by water and fungus. Depending on the type and degree of spalting, the wood varies from being beautiful to being totally useless—it has to be caught and halted at just the right stage. The greater part of this particular piece of spalted wood is really good for carving—everything is usable except about an inch or so (2 or 3cm) at the edge.

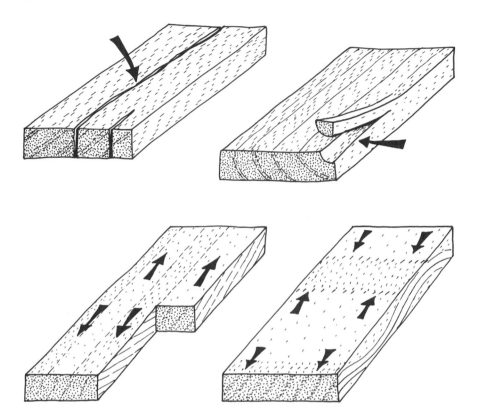

2–3   *Wood faults to be avoided. (Top left) A shake caused by too rapid drying. This particular type of shake is characterized by splits on the board ends that run through the wood in the direction of the grain. (Top right) Splits at and around the middle of the tree—around the pith—are termed* cup *shakes. (Bottom left) A streaked grain pattern caused by the spiral growth in the annual rings. Such a wood might well be very difficult to carve. (Bottom right) Undulating, or fiddleback, is due to the grain running alternately upwards and downwards. If you desire to show an undulating grain, then fiddleback can be beautiful; if its presence is unexpected, then it's a nuisance.*

Checks and Shakes

If a length of sawn timber is in any way cracked or split, then it is described as having a check or shake (see **2–3**). Separations that occur throughout the length of a log are termed *through shakes*; cracks that show on the end of log sections—meaning around the edge—are described as *star*

shakes (see **2–4**); cracks that occur at the center of log sections are described as *heart shakes* (see **2–5**).

Since a crack or split is usually an indicator that the wood will somehow or other be a problem, our advice is to look for another piece.

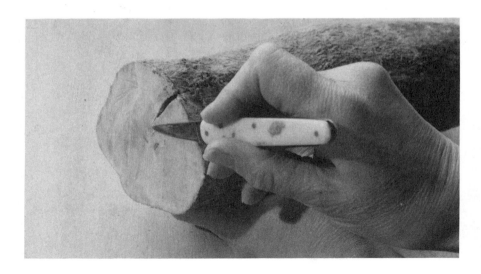

2–4   *A split caused by too rapid drying. Since this particular piece of boxwood is most certainly going to be a problem—with the crack widening and travelling along the length of the grain—we have decided to just let it be for a year and see how it ages.*

2-5 *This heart and star shake has rendered the end foot or so of this piece of wood essentially useless. However, since it only travels along the tree for a short distance, it might be that the greater part of the wood can be used.*

Decay

Although decay—meaning mould and fungi as seen on standing trees and sawn wood—does sometimes result in the wood having the most beautiful colors and patterns, it is, for the most part, clear evidence that the wood is useless for woodcarving (see **2-6**). For example, when we foolishly said yes to a piece of ash that had a yellowish stain on one face and felt a bit soft along one edge, we found that it was soft and rotten at the heart and totally useless for carving.

2-6 *This particular piece of wood has insect holes and fungi, making it particularly useful as fuel for our work-shop fire, but not for wood-carving.*

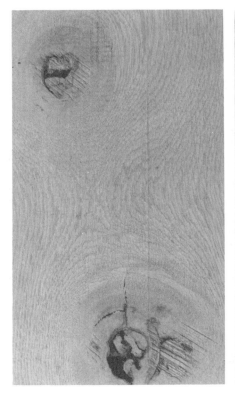

2–7 *Both sides of the same board. Although this oak board is about 2in (5cm) thick, the knots are going to be a problem. We may use the interesting bit in the middle, but the rest is scrap.*

If a piece of wood looks in any way to be spongy, has an odd smell, is stained, has holes, or whatever, our advice is either to cut out the bad areas and use the rest or, better still, to go for another piece of wood.

Knots

Knots are termed dead, hollow, loose, spiked, encased, and many other local names besides (see **2–7** and **2–8**). They tend to be difficult to carve, so avoid them if possible.

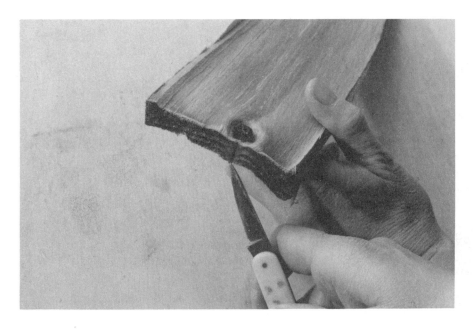

2–8 *If you look closely, you will see that this knot—once totally enclosed and hidden from view—shows itself on the sawn end as a ripple or fault in the grain. If we had spotted it earlier, we could, perhaps, have used the hole as a feature in one of our carved decoys.*

Trees into Timber

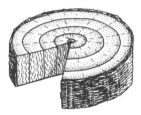

The growing tree is full of water. If we were to cut down a tree and weigh it—lets say that it weighs ten tons—then as like as not, half—at least five tons—of that weight would be made up of water. If we were then to take the green wood—meaning wet wood straight from the newly felled tree—and make a carving, then as the wood dried out, the carving would crack, move, warp, shrink, bend, and otherwise make a mess of our work.

But how is it—you may ask—that some carvers, particularly folk, ethnic, or tribal, use green wood? Early American settlers, it seems, were also able to cut and carve furniture and domestic woodware straight from the tree (see **2–9**). Well, think about the conditions under which the "green" items were put to use: cold, dark, drafty shelters, with plenty of moisture, perhaps even water riveting down the walls, hardly any light or heat, a stiff breeze blowing in through unglazed openings. These conditions are very nearly perfect for long, slow natural seasoning. Nowadays, of course, just the opposite is the case: the conditions of our dry, 'hot, relatively airtight homes are damaging for wood that is in any way green or half-seasoned.

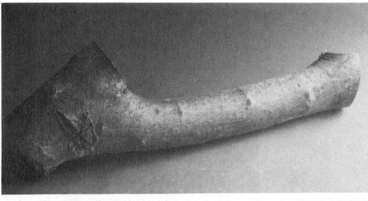

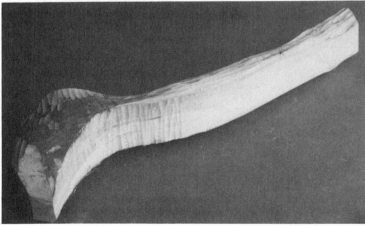

2–9 *The stages showing how we have carved a water dipper from a piece of apple wood. This unpromising section sawn from an old apple tree resulted in a very attractive carving. We cut the tree down in late summer/early autumn, cut it into short sections, and let them season for a year.*

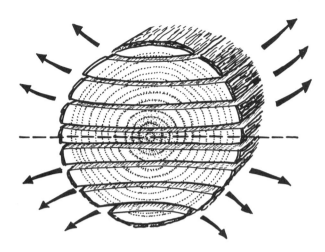

2–10 *Shrinkage and warping. Once the tree has been cut down, converted into planks, and generally relieved of tension, there is a tendency for the wood to dry out and warp. Although this drawing has been exaggerated, you can see that the heartwood contracts evenly and not as much as the sapwood.*

Cutting and Seasoning

Long before the wood reaches the carver, it is first cut into suitable size sections, and then dried and preshrunk. That is to say, the wood is converted into sawn timber, and seasoned (see **2–10**).

Sawing The shape, size, and grain patterns of the wood—meaning the wood that we eventually get to use in our workshops—is determined by the way the tree is sliced up (see **2–11**). For example, the log might be cut "through and through" with a series of parallel cuts—plain sawn—to make a stack of planks, or it might be cut into quarters, with each quarter then being sawn through so as to produce planks—quarter sawn—or then again planks can be cut off the side so as to finish up with a huge balk, or beam, of heartwood at the center. There are, in fact, dozens of methods of converting the tree into timber; each method has had its traditional use to produce suitable wood of such and such specific shape, pattern, and profile (see **2–12** and **2–13**).

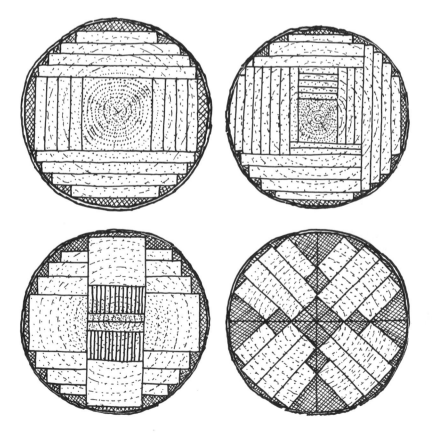

2–11 *Converting the tree into timber. Although there are many traditional ways of sawing up a tree, much depends on the type, size, and shape of the tree, and the intended use. (Top left) This method—termed* boxed heart—*results in a situation where there is a good beam at the center and all the boards are free from heartwood. (Top right) In this pattern for sawing plain American oak, it's plain to see that, by disregarding the medullary rays, there is a good beam at the center and a selection of boards and planks. (Bottom left) This traditional pattern, typically used by village carpenters and carvers, results in a good selection of different-size timbers. (Bottom right) Although this method of quarter sawing—as used for small-dimension logs—results in a good batch of timbers, there is also a lot of waste.*

2–12 *Waney wood with the bark attached. This particular piece of wood has limited use. Even when the bark is removed the outer wood is going to be too soft.*

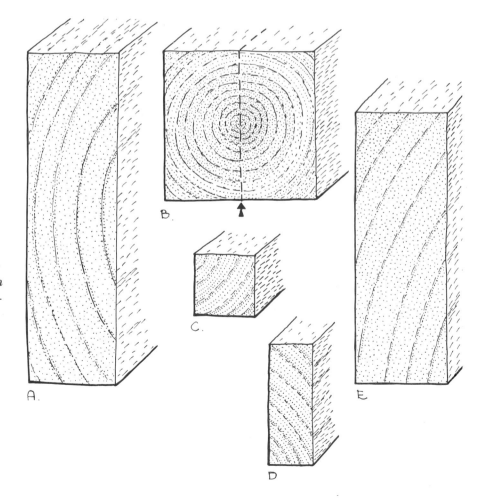

2–13 *Converted softwood sections: (A) Plank—at an average dimension of 3in × 11in (7.6cm × 28cm); (B) Baulk— called a half timber when cut in half—usually larger than 4½in (11.4cm) square; (C) Scantling—small stuff at about 2in to 4in (5.1cm to 10.2cm) square; (D) Board— up to 2in (5.1cm) thick and over 4in (10.2cm) wide; (E) Deal—averages out at about 3in (7.6cm) thick and 9in (23cm) wide.*

Stacking   Once the timber has been sawn, it is stacked so that there is a good air flow between the layers. This is achieved by "stickering" the stack—meaning the neighboring boards are spaced with little square sections of wood called skids or sticks (see **2–14**).

If you decide to stack and sticker your own wood—either wood you have sawn or wood you have purchased green—then make sure that the site is clear of grass, the top of the stack is covered with a sheet of ply weighted down with rocks or concrete blocks, and the stack is under partial cover. Allow about 12 months' seasoning for every 1in (2.5cm) of board thickness.

Seasoning   Throughout the seasoning stage, the free water is removed from cell cavities within the wood until the moisture content is in equilibrium, or you might say balanced, with the surrounding environment.

There are two ways that sawn wood can be seasoned; it can either be very carefully spaced and stacked—as already described—or it can be spaced and stacked on a trolley, slid into an oven, and kiln-dried with hot air and steam.

Both methods of seasoning have their problems and drawbacks. It's a question of time and money: slow air-dried wood at low cost, or fast kiln-drying at high cost. Another point to consider is that while air-dried timber still contains a fair amount of water—to the extent that it will continue to dry and shrink—kiln-dried timber is usually so over-dry that it actually takes up water and starts to expand.

For our purposes, possible consequences are that a carving made from air-dried wood might well continue to shrink and crack, whereas a carving made from kiln-dried might well expand and warp. With either choice, in most cases the movement is quite small and the cracking minimal.

All in all, we prefer, if possible, to go for wood that has been naturally seasoned and dried. What we usually do is bring the wood into our workshop, let it sit around for quite some time so that it continues to dry out and generally harden, and then eventually start carving (see **2–15**).

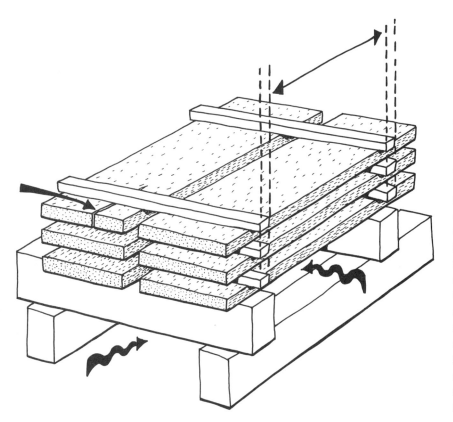

2–14   The seasoning procedure involves carefully stacking the sawn wood so that there is a good air flow and even drying. The skids, or stickers—meaning the strips of wood used as spacers—must be of uniform thickness and carefully aligned so that they are stacked in a column. Thin boards need skids about 12in (30.5cm) part, whereas thicker boards may be set with skids about 24in (61cm) apart. If cracks or splits appear at the end of the sawn boards, then the wood should be covered and/or the ends of the boards should be coated with paint, wax, or pitch.

Good Wood for Carving

It is important to be familiar with suitable woods for carving. Here we present an **A–Z list** of what each wood looks like, how it performs and finishes, along with some of our personal observations from using the wood. Each entry includes a parenthetical designation of where it is commonly found (Asia, Austr = Australia, Can = Canada, Eur = Europe, Jap = Japan, NZ = New Zealand, UK = United Kingdom, USA = United States of America).

Alder—red   Known also as western alder, Oregon alder, and one or two other names besides. Alder is a soft-grained, easy-to-work, pale-colored hardwood. Traditionally it was used by native people of North America—and later by settlers—for bowls and dishes. Cuts to a good finish and is easy to polish.
(Can, Eur, UK, USA)

Apple   A dark, dense, close-grained hardwood—comes in small sizes, carves well, has a beautiful color, and takes a good polish.
(Eur, UK, USA)

Ash   A long-grained, tough hardwood. Very difficult to carve. From country to country the qualities and characteristics vary. Traditionally used for handles, poles, and sticks.
(Eur, Jap, UK, USA)

Basswood   Although basswood—sometimes confused with linden or lime (see *Linden*)—is classified as a hardwood, it is in fact a wonderfully easy and satisfying wood to carve. Characteristically, it is pale cream to yellowish brown with a uniform fine texture. If you are a beginner to woodcarving and want to start with an easy-to-work wood, then this is a good wood to go for. Having made the point that lime/linden and basswood are different trees, their cutting characteristics are almost identical.
(Can, USA)

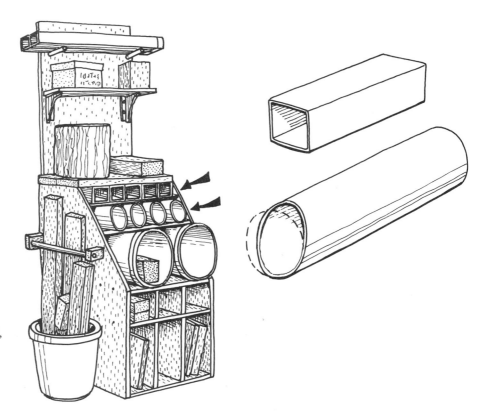

2–15   Storage is always a problem—the wood always seems to be too big, too small, too long, too heavy, and always too much. The setup shown may suit your workshop situation.

Beech   A heavy, inexpensive hardwood with yellowish sapwood and reddish heartwood. This is one of our favorite woods—it's very pleasant to carve, with a good range of colors.
(Austr, Can, Eur, Jap, NZ, UK, USA)

Birch   A pale hardwood used traditionally for making turned and carved chairs. Known variously around the world as yellow (*Betula*) birch, paper birch, and many other names besides. A very popular wood in Scandinavia and America—much favoured for small domestic woodware such as bowls, dishes, and troughs.
(Can, Eur, USA)

Box   A beautiful, butter-smooth hardwood with a hard, dense grain. It cuts to a polished hard-edged finish, only comes in very small sizes, and is very tricky to carve. Traditionally used for printing blocks and fancy carving, it takes the most amazing detail.
(Eur, UK)

Canary (American whitewood)   A yellowish soft wood—but classed as a hardwood—even-grained and knot-free. Sometimes known as yellow poplar, tulip wood, canoe wood, saddle wood, and other names besides. Although it is often described as being easy to carve, we find that it is a bit ragged and rough.
(Can, USA)

Cedar   A fine, straight-grained, rich red softwood with a pleasing aromatic odor when freshly sawn. There are many types—with prefix names like Alaska, Atlantic, red, white, pencil, and so on. Although cedar is a wonderful wood for carving—we particularly like pencil cedar—there are so many types that you really need to try out the piece before buying. Be very careful when ordering that you don't get one of the difficult-to-carve and endangered African types.
(Can, Eur, UK, USA)

Cherry   A close-grained, pleasant-to-work, red/brown hardwood—good for small projects. Carves well—can be brought to a high-shine polished finish. Usually has a rich red color, with some parts fading into pink and cream. Cherry, generally black cherry, is considered to be a good wood for carving—ideal for beginners.
(Can, Eur, Jap, UK, USA)

Chestnut   A brown hardwood—very much like English oak in that the grain is firm and compact. It carves well. When we talk about chestnut, we mean the American or Spanish chestnut, not the horse chestnut, which is a different species. Chestnut is good to carve, but quite difficult to find. American chestnut was attacked by a blight and exists almost solely as standing dead trees or old timber.
(Eur, UK, USA)

Cottonwood   Cottonwood—also known as eastern cottonwood, swamp cottonwood, black cottonwood, balsam poplar, or simply as poplar—is a plentiful, greyish white, light-in-weight hardwood that is generally good for carving. Cottonwood has a straight grain and cuts to a slightly fluffy finish.
(Can, Eur, USA)

Elm   A hardwood, known variously around the world as red elm, nave elm, water elm, swamp elm, Japanese elm, and many other names besides. Elm is characterized by being coarse-textured, tough, and straight-grained. It ranges in color from pale cream to reddish brown. Although elm is relatively difficult to work, it cuts to a good, smooth finish, takes detail, and polishes well.

In America and England, elm was once considered to be the primary wood for making just about everything. Now, of course, elm is in short supply because of two diseases, Dutch Elm and phloem necrosis. A good wood if you can find it.
(Can, Eur, USA)

Fir   A softwood known variously as the true firs, balsam fir, Oregon pine, red pine, yellow pine, noble fir, white fir, and many other names. True firs are creamy white to pale brown. Douglas fir is characterized by being straight-grained, reddish brown in young trees and yellowish brown in old trees, with a fair scattering of large-size knots. Although fir is difficult to work, the resultant carvings exhibit an exciting grain pattern. (Can, UK, USA)

Holly   Instantly recognized as a growing tree, holly is a hardwood that is typified by being smooth, close-grained, and ivory-white. Being the whitest wood available, it is much favored by woodcarvers who are looking to work small, detailed sculptures. If it is left in the sun as a log, however, it soon fades to a dull grey. (Eur, UK, USA)

Larch   A softwood that is characterized by being straight-grained, resinous, and of a uniform texture. It ranges from white-pink to orange-red. A very attractive grain, difficult—but exciting—to carve; similar to Douglas fir. (Eur, UK, USA)

Linden/lime   For many traditionalists in Europe, the UK, and America, linden—widely known as lime—is the primary hardwood for fine carving. Linden is a family of trees—*Tiliaceae*—of which the genus *Tilia* is generally termed linden, native in temperate regions. The North American linden is sometimes called "basswood" or "whitewood," leading to a lot of confusion, since many woodcarvers are left thinking that lime, linden, and basswood are all one and the same. In fact, in one of our early woodcarving books, we mistakenly state that they *are* one and the same.

Although we are being sticklers here, we have to admit that the light, close-grained, buttercream white wood of linden/lime, while differing slightly in strength, is, in almost all respects, identical in cutting characteristics to basswood. Knot-free, easy-to-cut linden/lime is a really good wood for beginners. It was/is famous for being the wood used by Grinling Gibbons (1648–1721), the English woodcarver who in 1714 was appointed master carver in wood to George I and is well known for work on great cathedrals, the chapel at Windsor, and great houses such as Burleigh, Chatsworth, and the ceiling at Petworth. (Eur, UK, USA)

Maple—soft   Known variously as red maple, soft maple, and simply maple, this hardwood is straight-grained and fine-textured. It ranges in color from cream to red-brown. It is much easier to carve and work than the wood commonly known as rock or hard maple. Cuts and polishes to a good finish. (Can, Eur, USA)

Maple—hard   Known also as rock maple, sugar maple, hard maple, field maple, bigleaf maple, and by quite a few other names, hard maple is close-grained and uniform in texture. It ranges from nearly white to cream and reddish brown. Although hard maple is difficult to carve, it does cut to a wonderful crisp, smooth finish. (Can, UK, USA)

Norway spruce   Known also as European white-wood or even as European spruce, this wood is even-textured, straight-grained, and has a minimum of knots. It works well and cuts to a good finish. It is usually a pale yellow-brown. (Eur)

Oak   Although there are many varieties of oak—English oak, American red and white oak, Baltic oak, Japanese oak, to name but a few—all with slightly differing color and grain characteristics, none has such a long history of usage for woodcarving, perhaps, as English oak. It has been said that oak is the oldest of woods known to be used for woodcarving.

Generally speaking, oak is straight-grained, medium to coarse in texture, with a color that grades from white and pale yellow to pink, brown, and red. Although common tradition has it that oak is difficult to carve—like iron or stone—from our experience we have found that it works readily and cuts to a clean finish. However, there is a tendency for the wood to move and twist, and it is difficult to carve detail. All in all, we think that every beginner needs to have a go with oak—just for the experience! (Asia, Eur, Jap, UK, USA)

Pine—eastern white   Sometimes confused with Ponderosa pine and western white, and also known variously as yellow pine, Quebec pine, Weymouth pine, soft pine, and quite a few other names besides. Eastern white pine is a straight-grained, even-textured softwood that is very good for carving. If you are a beginner and looking for a relatively inexpensive wood, a wood that cuts cleanly and takes a polish, then this is the one for you.
(Can, USA)

Pine—general   And just in case you aren't already confused with regard to pine, there are at least thirty botanical designations for pine, plus seventy general and local names. That said, pine is the most widely spread softwood. It grows in vast northern zones throughout North America, in Scotland, Norway, and Europe to Asia. The various pine types are different in character—with some being smooth and easy to carve, whereas others are ragged and almost impossible. The best approach is to try out local easy-to-find varieties, and then take it from there.
(Asia, Can, Eur, Jap, NZ, UK, USA)

Pine—western white   Known also as Idaho white pine, this softwood is very similar in character to yellow or white pine. In fact, there are so many overlapping names for pine that we are all confused. All you need to know is that it is a straight-grained, yellowish white pine that is readily carved. It's particularly good for large built-up figures that are going to be painted.
(Can, USA)

Sequoia   Sometimes called California redwood, this softwood and its close cousin the giant sequoia are special, if for no other reason than their vital statistics. For example, some trees are more than 4000 years old, they grow to a diameter of 30ft (9.15m) at the base, and they reach heights greater than 300ft (91.5m). Straight-grained and reddish brown in color, the texture varies from being fine to ragged. Although it is generally good to carve, heartwood is sometimes brittle and weak along its length—so much so that it can be snapped like a carrot.
(USA)

Spruce—Sitka spruce   Sometimes also known locally as silver spruce, tideland spruce, western spruce, and so on, this is a nonresinous, cream-white wood with a straight-grained, even texture. Sometimes good for carving—depending on the piece and species.
(Can, UK, USA)

Sycamore   Also called Sycamore plane, great maple, buttonwood, and planetree, this is a fine, even-textured hardwood with a characteristic yellow-white color and a lustrous surface. If you want to carve bowls and dishes for use in the kitchen, then sycamore can't be bettered; it works well, cuts to a good finish, is easy to clean, resists warping and splitting, and, best of all, is completely safe and nontoxic.
(Asia, Eur, UK)

Yew   A softwood, also called common yew, English yew, or European yew. In the context of English and European woodcarving, yew has a long history of being featured in folklore with the attribution of mystical qualities; a longbow made from yew had special powers, a door made from yew would protect the house from the "evil eye," and so forth. From our viewpoint, although yew is a beautiful wood to cut and carve, we don't use it, simply because it is *toxic*. All in all, it's a very decorative wood, with a rich pale cream to orange-red color.
(Eur, UK)

Chapter 3

KNIFE, AXE, AND ADZE

The knife, axe, and adze are three of the oldest tools known to humans. When someone discovered that a flake struck from a flint nodule produced an instant cutting edge, it was certainly a major development—like inventing the combustion engine, or splitting the atom. And much later, when someone mounted the flint in a wooden handle, it was really a breakthrough in technology and an enormous increase in efficiency. And while the basic concept—of knife, axe, and adze—has remained immutable, its inception immediately altered the dynamic of power and prestige.

Tools and Usage

And so the story goes on from a flint held in the hands to cutting edges made of shell and then copper. Later it was the iron blade as the metal of choice. With the discovery of adding carbon to create a hardened alloy, steel proved to be altogether the most efficient cutting material.

Knives

Of all the tools employed in woodcarving, the knife is, at one and the same time, the most widely used, the most versatile, and yet the most underrated (see **3-1**). We say this because although woodcarvers have traditionally used—and still use—knives for a whole range of tasks, many new to the craft tend to think of the knife, if at all, as an inferior tool used by people of limited means. This way of thinking is, perhaps, even encouraged by the tool manufacturers, who usually feature a single craft-type knife with a throwaway blade in a metal handle.

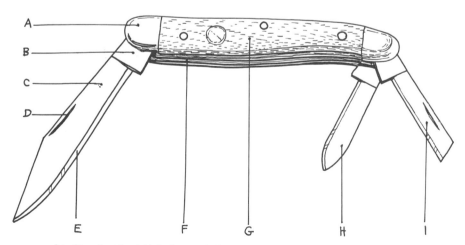

3–1 *The all-purpose whittling knife. (A) bolster; (B) tang; (C) master blade; (D) opening slot; (E) cutting edge; (F) lining or case; (G) handle cover; (H) small blade; (I) small blade. A knife of this character needs to be well built from top-quality materials. Make sure that the blades are firm and well pivoted.*

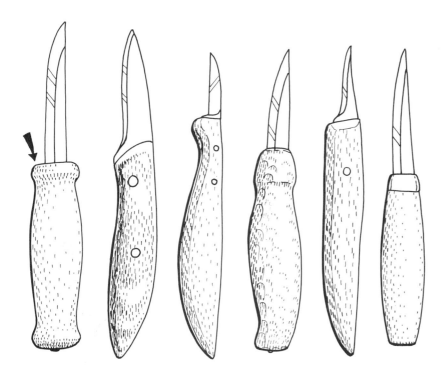

3–2   Knife handles. A carving knife must be a good, comfortable nonslip fit in your hand—no matter what grip you use; it shouldn't slip around or have rough edges. Be wary of handles that flare out towards the blade—certainly the handle does need to have a slight flare to stop your hand from slipping (see the arrow), but if it is too big, then it's likely to get in the way. (Left to right) Frost laminated-steel knife from Sweden; KGH custom knife from USA; Rick Butz knife from Germany; Willie Sundqvist knife with a hand-carved handle from Sweden; Lamp Band knife from USA; sloyd-type knife from Sweden.

Well, the good news is that there are many beautiful knife types out there (see **3–2** and **3–3**). There are drawknives that are used for shaping curved profiles, hooked and crooked knives that are used for carving hollows, knives for whittling, knives for chip carving, small knives for detailing, Swedish knives with bone handles for general work, Japanese knives for whittling miniatures,

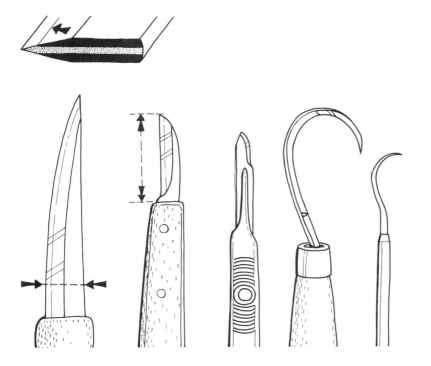

3–3   Knife blade shapes. (Top) Best-quality blades that hold a good edge and stay sharper longer are usually laminated, with a layer of hard carbon steel between layers of mild steel. If you look closely at such a blade, you should be able to see the line of the lamination running along the face of the bevel. (Left to right) general-purpose roughing-out blade shape with a width of about ½in (13mm); round-ended detail knife with a blade about 1¼in (32mm) long and ¼in (6mm) wide; surgical scalpel for cutting fine details; hooked blade for cutting hollows; dental type knife, sometimes called a pick, for detailing miniatures.

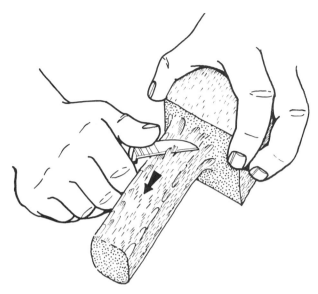

3–4 *Holding the knife. The thumb-pushing cut is used when you are cutting away from your body. In use, your elbows are tucked into your sides to brace, brake, and generally control the extent of the cut.*

and so on. Knives are very efficient low-cost carving tools (see **3–4**, **3–5**, **3–6**, **3–7**, **3–8**, and **3–9**). And even more exciting is that with each of these knife types—that is, within each of these areas of knife usage—there are many knives made for a single, specific task.

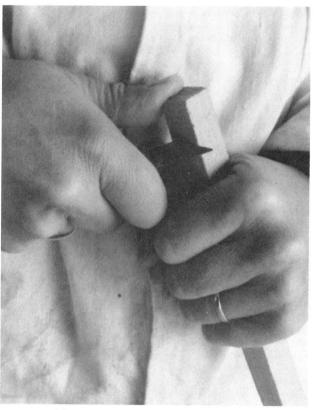

3–5 *Holding the knife. The classic thumb-paring cut uses the thumb as a lever to increase the efficiency of the stroke. Note how the general stance— with the arms and workpiece being held tight against the body—ensures that the cut is totally controlled.*

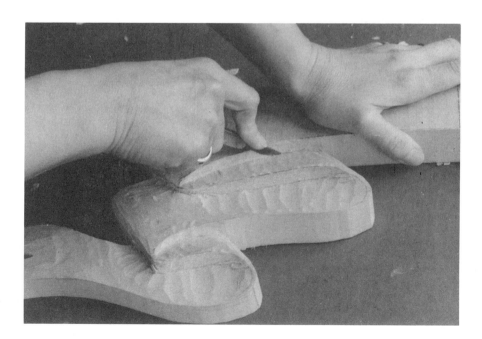

3–6 *Holding the knife. The grasping and dragging cut— used for marking out and setting-in—enables the carver to exert maximum pressure.*

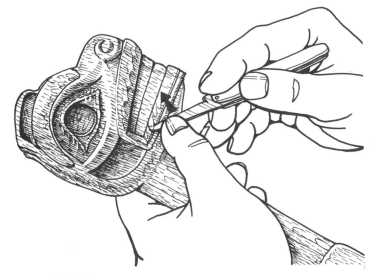

3–7   *Holding the knife. This thumb-pushing cut is managed by holding and pivoting the knife in one hand, while at the same time pushing against the back of the blade with the other hand. A good cut for working small details.*

3–8   *Holding the knife. An extension of the thumb-pushing cut is to have both hands braced and linked. Although this way of working increases both the efficiency and the control, it can only be managed if the workpiece is relatively large and held secure by a clamp.*

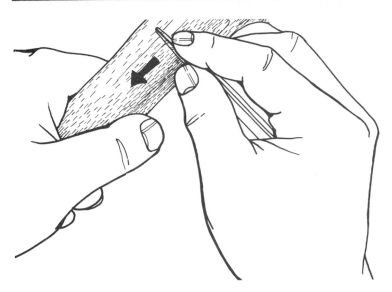

3–9   *Holding the knife. To use a knife to scrape a surface down to a smooth finish, hold the blade so that it is more or less at right angles to the surface being worked, and drag it backwards and forward in line with the grain. If the grain cuts up rough, then try sharpening the knife and/or scraping at an angle to the run of the grain.*

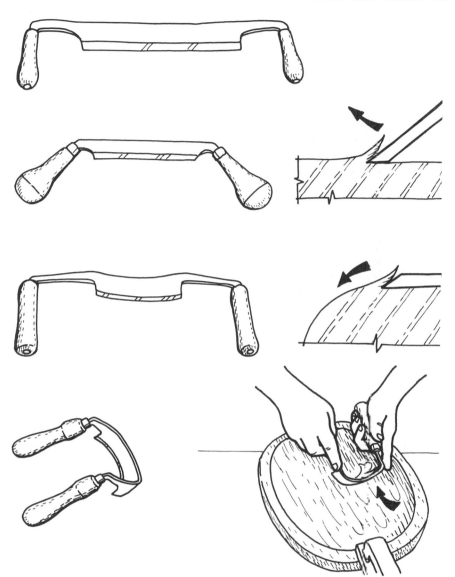

3–10 *The drawknife. If you are working on a good-size piece and you want to remove waste relatively fast, then the drawknife is an amazingly efficient tool. The only thing is, of course, that since the drawknife needs to be held in both hands, the workpiece must be held secure in a clamp or holdfast. (Top left) Straight knives for general work. (Middle left) The slightly curved knife is used for light cuts and for finishing a flat surface. (Bottom, left and right) The deep-scooping knife—sometimes called a scorp or an in-shave—is used primarily for finishing deep hollows. (Top right) Be mindful when you are working with a single-bevel knife that the tool always rides away from the bevel. For example, if you have the bevel facing down, then the tool will ride up, and if you have the bevel facing up, then the tool will ride down.*

The drawknife alone includes straight ones with a single bevel used for carving chair legs, curved ones for cutting concave hollows on chair seats, and deep U-shaped ones for carving the inside of barrels (see **3–10**).

Most beginners experience difficulties when they first come to use a knife—usually because the tool is not top quality. Our advice is to stay away from the general-purpose craft-type knives and to search out a few quality tools. Get the right knife, and you will have one of the best of all wood-carving tools—a friend for life.

Axes and Hatchets

The axe and the hatchet are both striking and cutting tools that perform in much the same way as a hammer and chisel. The distinctive difference between axes and hatchets is simple enough: axes

are generally held and used with two hands, the handles being long and tapered, whereas the hatchet is used with one hand, the handle being much shorter in length.

Both the narrow and broad axe are used in woodcarving (see **3–11**), the choice usually being affected by the size and character of the wood that is being worked. Although there are all manner of axe head types—for example, the overall shape of an American axe being quite different from say a Scotch axe—the cutting edge of an axe is characterized by being convex in side profile, with a bevel on both sides of the blade.

The convex or curved edge performs in much the same way as a wedge—meaning the leading edge of the convex curve initiates a progressive splitting cut. If we were able to study the cutting action of the axe in slow motion, we would see that the leading edge of the convex curve first separates the fibres of the wood, and then the rest of the curve progressively opens up the wood from the center outward.

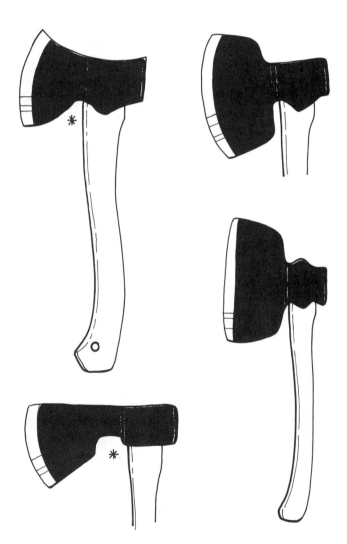

3–11 *When the carver's axe is being used for detail work—meaning when you want to work with a steady carving stroke—the scooped out "throat" at the back of the head allows you to hold the handle safely, high up against the head. The broad-head axe is a particularly good tool for removing large areas of waste.*

3–12 *Axe handling. When you are using the axe for medium-size hewing, make sure that the block is at a good height and stable; have your legs set slightly apart, and braced so that your in-path-of-swing knee is set back at a distance from the block; make sure that the hand holding the wood is well clear of the swing; and be warned—working with an axe is one of those tasks that requires maximum concentration.*

Being mindful that there are hundreds of axe types, with just about every district within a region favoring its own particular shape, the most important point is that the woodcarver's axe is primarily a wedge-like tool that is used to split the fibres of the wood. Certainly there are instances where you might think that the axe is being used to cut across the grain—for example, when the carver is working on the back of a bowl, or cutting a flat face on a log—but what he is actually doing is running the blade into the wood in a long shearing action. The blade enters the wood at an angle to the run of the grain and then shears through the fibres.

The shape and form of the axe handle is of particular interest. Not only is the handle nearly always oval in section, with the thin part of the oval shape on the underside, but, more than that, it is gently curved and tapered along its length, having a thickness near the head and a slight swelling at the hand end. The oval cross section, the long slow curve, and the delicate end shape all enable the axe to be twisted and manipulated while it is being swung. Unlike, say, a hammer—which is a single-action tool—the axe is designed to be used for all manner of shearing, slanting, and glancing blows.

In use, the woodcarver usually works with one hand doing the holding, while the other hand is variously sliding up and down, releasing, regripping, guiding the axe to its mark, easing the head from the cut, and getting ready to rerun the stroke (see **3–12**).

Adzes

Although many woodcarvers tend to think of the adze as being a rather old-fashioned, limited tool—best reserved for its traditional use by furniture makers, house builders, ship builders,

wheelwrights, and coopers, with each discipline using maybe three or four designs—it is, in fact, a tool that potentially has a very wide use in woodcarving.

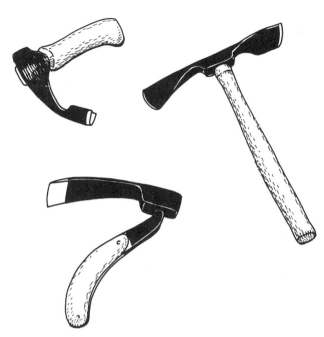

3–13   Adze types. (Top left) Gouge adze—used for hollowing small bowls. (Willie Sundqvist, Sweden) (Right) Multipurpose axe–adze—with a 2in (51mm) wide gouge blade, a 1½in (38mm) curved chisel/axe blade, and a 12in (30.5cm) hickory handle. (USA) (Bottom) A hollowing adze with a 3in (76mm) wide gouge No. 7 sweep profile. The long tapered head and the hooked shape enable the carver to make a scooping cut without the edge binding. (Italy)

The woodcarver's adze looks very much like an axe, the only real difference being that the cutting edge is set at an angle to the handle. Of course the shape and size of adzes vary, some having very short handles and long heads, and others having huge, spade-like heads and long handles; but overall the adze looks like a hybrid of an axe and a hoe (see **3–13**).

An adze may seem to be no more than a blade fixed to the end of a long handle, but the wonderful thing is that the length and shape of the handle, and the way it is swung from the wrist or shoulder, increase the blade's efficiency many times over. In use, the adze is swung, with the effect that the wood is scooped away as shell-like curls of waste. The cutting action of the adze—like a swinging, scooping pendulum—results in the blade leaving a characteristic dappled or rippled finish.

Beginner's Workout

Using a Straight Knife

If you are interested in using the knife for small woodcarving such as whittling, then there are two things that you are going to have to master. First and foremost you must know the basic holds, and secondly you must learn about how and when to use a stop-cut. This is a wonderfully easy exercise; all you need is a small piece of wood about 6in (15cm) long and a good, sharp knife. We have chosen to use a piece of wood with a 1in (25mm) square section simply because our workshop is full of these, but you could just as well use a branch, a piece of dowel, or a chunk cut from a tree. Follow the sequential drawings and the captions in **3–14**, **3–15**, and **3–16**.

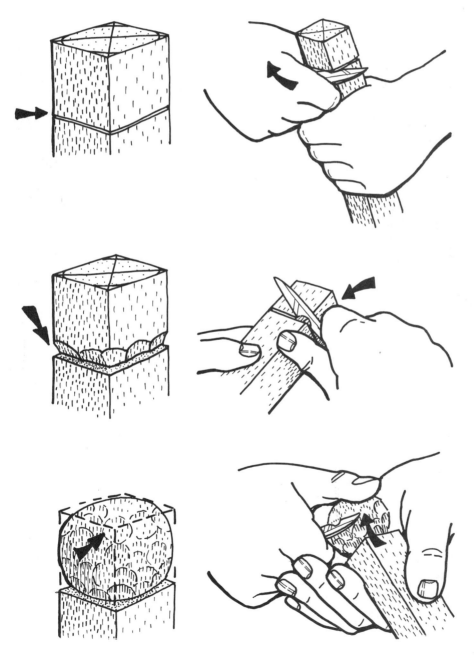

3–14 Knife handling exercises. (Top, left, and right) Making the stop-cut—having marked out the wood, take the wood in one hand and the knife in the other—both in a strong grasping grip—and run a single, deep cut into the wood. Use the thumb of the knife hand as a guide and for leverage. (Middle, left, and right) Run an angled slicing cut into the initial stop-cut to make a clear trench. Rerun the initial stop-cut and the angled cut several times around the wood until you get to the required depth. (Bottom, left, and right) Having defined the depth and breadth of the stop-cut, switch to holding the knife with a paring thumb-braced cut, and systematically whittle off the sharp shoulder of waste. Note how the act of linking hands and levering against the workpiece with your thumb ensures that the cutting procedure is both strong and safe.

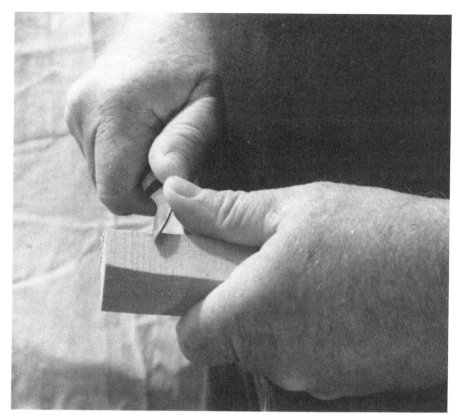

3–15 *The touching thumbs ensure that the cut has maximum control and leverage—the knife hand supplies the support, and the thumb of the hand holding the wood actually does the work.*

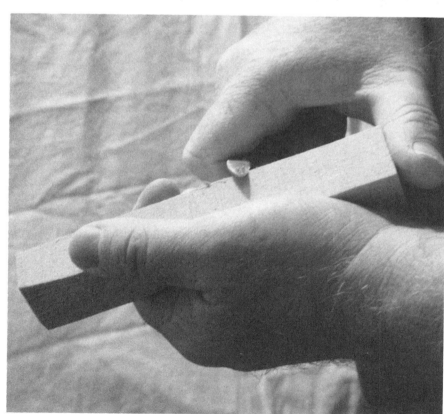

3–16 *The technique of holding the knife at a low angle to pare off long, thin slices only works if the hand holding the wood is behind the knife, and your elbows are tucked tight into your waist. It is the tight-braced elbows that make for a safe and controlled cut.*

Using a Small Hatchet

Most of us are familiar with a hatchet—its overall shape, size, and usage. Maybe you have used a hatchet at camp or to chop firewood.

This basic exercise takes you one step beyond the usual chopping and splitting cut in that it describes how to manage what we call the basic *shearing* cut. If you are interested in carving domestic wares, such as bowls, dishes, troughs, and small stools, then this is the exercise for you.

You need a half-round section split from a softwood log about 10in (25.4cm) in diameter and 12in (30.5cm) long; you need a small sharp hatchet; and you need a chopping block at a comfortable height. When you are searching out your wood, go for a piece that is freshly cut, straight-grained, and free of knots (see **3–17**).

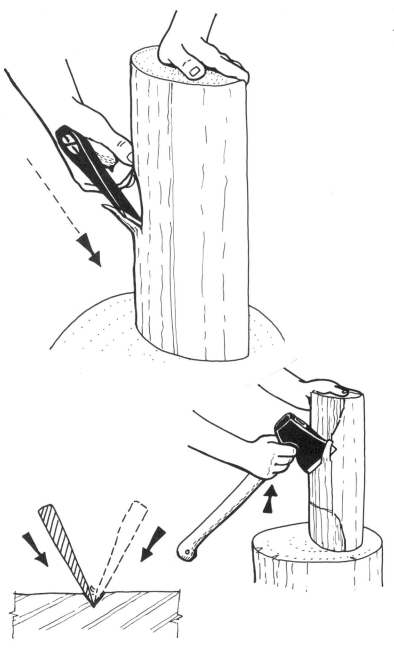

3–17 Axe handling exercises. First and foremost—before you start work—make sure that the block is at a good height and completely stable, and see to it that you and the workshop are in good, safe order. If your children want to watch—and it's good fun if they do—then make certain that they know the ground rules about sitting still and being quiet. Or to put it another way—you don't want any distractions, and they mustn't get in the way. (Top) The basic shearing cut is achieved by supporting the workpiece on the block, holding the axe high up the handle so that your hand is behind the head, and then working with a controlled cut. If the axe is sharp and the wood correctly angled, then the weight of the axe will do most of the work. If the workpiece vibrates in your hand to the extent that it sends shock waves up your arm, then it means either that the wood isn't in good contact with the block and/or the wood is being held at too low an angle. (Bottom right) If you want to make a bowl, trim off one end of the log, rerun the procedure on the other end, and then trim off the base. If you hold the handle with your hand tucked out of harm's way high up behind the head of the axe, and if you go for lots of small skimming cuts, then you will find that this is a swift, safe, and easy technique for shaping large forms. (Bottom left) If and when you come to cut across the grain—and this isn't as easy as a shaving cut—make sure that the axe is sharp, and then angle the cuts to remove a V-section slice of waste. If you find that the axe blows crush rather than cut, then the axe needs sharpening.

Using a Small Adze

If you used the small hatchet for the above exercise, then it follows that you are going to be interested in using the small hand adze for basic hollowing. In many ways this is one of the archetypal carving techniques. If you can clear a hollow with an adze, then a whole world of woodcarving is going to open up before you—bowls, troughs, spoons, toy boats, masks—the possibilities are endless. You need the same sort of half-round log as used in the axe exercise; you need a small gouge adze; and you need the chopping block at a comfortable height (see **3–18**).

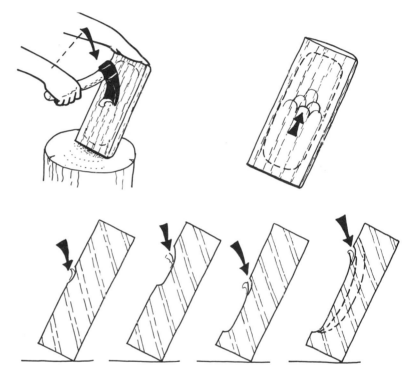

3–18 Adze handling exercises to hollow out a bowl shape. (Top left) Having marked out the area that you want to hollow, support the workpiece on the block, and have a few practice strokes with the adze. Aim to work out from the middle of the area that needs to be hollowed. (Top right) When you have got into the swing of using the adze, work out from the middle so that you are retreating towards the edge of the area that needs to be dished. If you are doing it right, your cuts should overlap—like fish scales or roof tiles. (Bottom, left to right) The left-to-right sequence of cuts is to cut out little-by-little from the middle at one end of the block, then reverse the block and rerun the procedure for the other end. This method of working not only ensures that you are cutting from high to low wood, but better yet, the backing-up cut is a way of making sure that the waste comes off as thin skims and slivers.

Chapter 4

CHIP CARVING

Chip carving is arguably one of the most beautiful techniques used by the woodcarver. It is a relatively simple process in which the surface of the wood—meaning the surface of a form that has already been carved and shaped—is organized into a grid, and then systematically nicked with an edge tool like a knife or chisel. The resultant cuts, usually triangular in section—in the form of small pockets or incised lines (see **4–1**) are grouped and arranged to create all manner of patterns (see **4–2**).

Unfortunately, when people think of chip carving, they usually have in mind the tourist-trade carvings that were produced in the late nineteenth and early twentieth centuries in such countries as Germany, Switzerland, and Russia. There is no denying that such chip carvings are beautifully crafted, wonderfully intricate, and altogether crisp, clean, and elaborate, but to our sensibility the ones for general sale are generally just too ordered and mechanical.

Perhaps we are being hard on nineteenth- and twentieth-century European chip carving, but if you really want to see chip carving at its most exciting, if you want to see chip carving that is dynamic, vigorous, and above all spontaneous, then you need to look to African and Oceanic tribal traditions and to European folk work that predates tourism (see **4–3**).

As to the roots of the craft, it has been suggested that chip carving traditionally formed a large part of African art—the technique being used to decorate everything from weapons and paddles to bowls and masks.

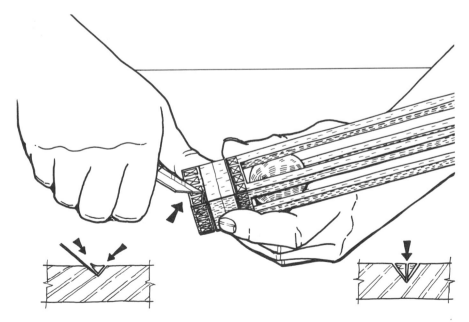

4–1 *This particular carving—a ball-in-a-cage puzzle—has been decorated with incised lines and triangular chip cuts. (Bottom left) The classic two-stroke incised line is used for shallow designs—the waste being removed with two angled cuts. (Bottom right) The three-stroke cut is used for a deeper V-section. The working procedure is to make the initial straight-down centerline stopcut, and follow through with two angled cuts.*

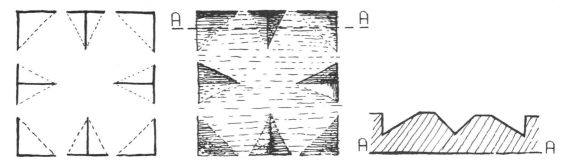

4–2 *(Left) With the hard lines representing straight-down stop-cuts, and the broken lines representing angled or slicing cuts, you can see that the corner pockets are created with three cuts—two straight down and one angled—whereas the side pockets are created with four cuts—two straight down and two at an angle. (Middle and right) The completed cut and the cross section.*

4–3 *English chest. Seen from the back with the lid open—with chip-carved designs—thought to be seventeenth century. Designs of this size and character would have been worked with the chisel as well as the knife. (Victoria and Albert Museum, London)*

Another school of thought suggests that the reasons behind chip carving being more or less a worldwide technique have to do with the fact than it is a fundamental woodcarving procedure. This same school of thought goes on to suggest that chip carving is therefore the ideal way for beginners to start carving.

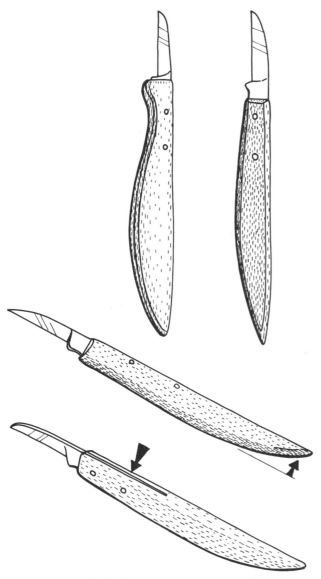

4–4 If you are looking for a good general-purpose knife, then a sheepsfoot might well suit your way of working. A knife of this type is characterized by having a short blade with a thumb notch for control and safety, and a tang running well into the handle. The best knives are fixed with rivets.

Tools and Usage

Although on the face of it, chip carving sounds a bit of a cinch when it comes to tools—because, after all, it can all be done with a single knife—you do need to pick your knives with care. We say this because the mistake most beginners make is to pick up a chunk of wood and the first knife that comes to hand, and then wind up disappointed when the whole thing doesn't work out easily. The point is that you can't, say, pick up a bit of pine and a kitchen knife, and then expect to do good work. The knotty pine is going to be uneven-grained and almost impossible to cut and the knife blade is going to be too pointed, too blunt, too springy, too dangerous to use, or all of these things.

As there are so many knife types on the market—some good, some wonderful, and some just average, in a wide price range with some of the best knives being relatively inexpensive—we decided, in all fairness, not to recommend particular knives, but rather to describe the various options available so that you can take it from there.

Sheepsfoot Knife

The sheepsfoot-style, general-purpose carving knife, as marketed by various USA woodcarving catalogs, is characterized by having a short down-turned blade with a straight bevel edge, and a long, good-to-hold handle (see **4–4**). These knives are designed primarily to be used with a thumb-paring, clenching or grasping hold. The knife is held in one hand—gripped with three fingers wrapped around the handle, the index finger being braced on the workpiece and the thumb pushing against the handle—while the other hand applies pressure, steadying and guiding the cut. Of course, the hold will change slightly depending on the carver and whether or not the blade is being pulled or pushed; the design of the blade will vary depending on the manufacturer, but broadly speaking the long handle and the short blade enable the carver to exert maximum pressure with minimum effort (see **4–5**).

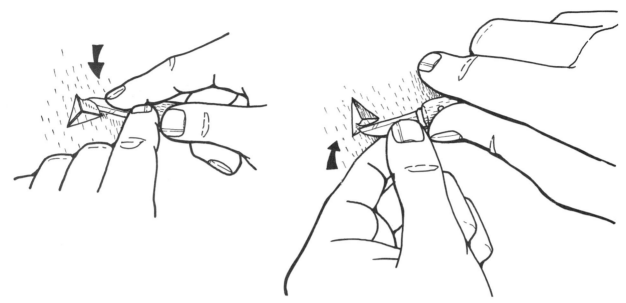

4–5   Using the sheepsfoot knife to make the classic six-cut triangular chip or pocket. (Left) Having first made the initial three straight-down-into-the wood cuts, remove the one side of the triangle with a pulling cut. In use, the knife is held and pulled with one hand, and supported and controlled with the other. The index finger of the left hand acts as a brake. (Right) When you come to slice away from your body, have your two hands linked and braced, so that the cut is tight and controlled.

Skew-Bladed Chip Knife

Described rather confusingly as a "cutting" knife, this particular type of knife is characterized by having a wide blade, a bevel set at an angle—skew—across the end of the blade, and a long, round-ended handle (see **4–6**). This knife is designed to be held with the butt of the handle pushed hard into the palm of the hand, and with the index finger of the same hand extended along the back of the blade. In use, the knife is pushed or stabbed in much the same way as a chisel. The shape of the blade and the set of the bevel allow the carver to go for all manner of grips and holds without fear of running any fingers against the cutting edge.

Knives of this type and character come in many designs, blade shapes ranging from long and narrow with the bevel at an acute angle to wide blades with the bevel set at less of an angle—almost like a chisel. It is important to note that, when chip carvings got to be bigger in scale, and when they were worked on tough woods like oak—as in the chip-carved roundels on English medieval chests—then the carvers tended to use chisels rather than knives. The techniques were the same; they simply needed bigger and stronger tools to make bigger and deeper cuts.

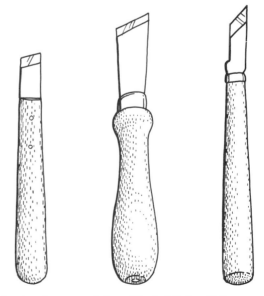

4–6   A selection of skew-bladed "chisel" knives.

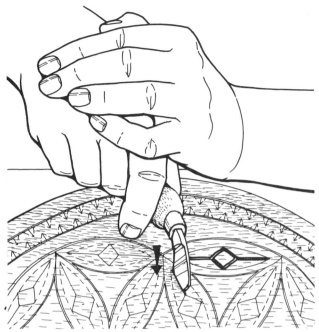

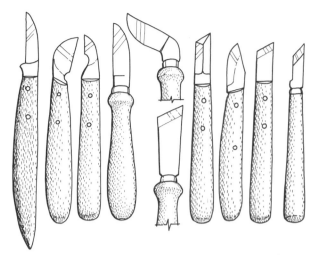

4–8 *A set of ten chip-carving knives. The blade names/types are: (left to right) sheepsfoot, large chip, small chip, spear; (top) crooked; (bottom) large skew, three-edge skew, sabre, small skew, fine skew.*

4–7 *The offset or crooked knife is used with a two-handed dragging stroke.*

Offset Knife

Although at first sight this curious-looking knife may seem puzzling and perhaps unusable—its blade elbowing out from the handle—it is, in fact, a very efficient easy-to-use tool. In essence, the angled offset blade is designed so that the knife can be both stabbed and pulled. For example, in use, the lines can be first set-in by making a straight-down dragging cut—one hand holding and guiding and the other hand supplying downward pressure (see **4–7**)—and then the same knife can be used flat—at a low angle—to the wood to slice out the individual chips.

Knife Sets

Any number of chip-carving knife sets are also available in a whole range of combinations. One set has four knives as already described plus a veiner gouge and a V-tool, another set has ten knives, another has three knives, and so on.

Our considered advice, if you are a beginner, is to start off by getting two medium-priced knives—a stab knife with a skew blade and a cutting knife for slicing out the waste (see **4–8**). Don't worry too much about the look of the han-dles or the sales pitch, just make sure that the blades are made from quality laminated steel and that the handles are comfortable to hold. We prefer natural, carved, plain wood handles—ones without an applied finish—because they are good to hold and are nonslip. The country of origin is not very important.

While you are getting your knives, you also need a couple of small sharpening stones—a medium-grade and a fine—and a leather strop.

Designing

We have noticed that beginners tend to shy away from chip carving; we suspect it is because they think it involves a lot of geometry to work out the designs. All that's needed are a few simple geometric tricks, a pencil, a straightedge, and a pair of compasses. Setting out designs is straightforward; each step follows from the last. How else do you think its use would have become so widespread?

If you can draw a circle with a compass and a straight line with a pencil and ruler, then chip carving designs are easy! Following the steps in the drawings will give you some idea of what is involved (see **4–9** and **4–10**).

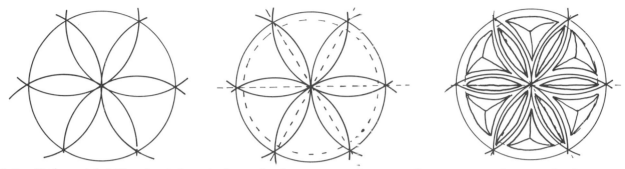

4–9 *(Left to right) The classic hex circle can be drawn out with a pair of compasses and a straightedge. The working stages: having first drawn a circle, stay with the same radius and work around the circumference drawing out the part-circle arcs; once you have drawn the six-petal flower, draw the dotted guide cuts in freehand; finally, mark in the position of all the lines that go to make up the pockets.*

4–10 *How the basic hex circle—as already described—can be repeated to make a complex design. (Top) The basic grid is drawn out with the compass fixed at the same radius. (Bottom—left to right) Use the basic grid and a series of freehand lines to mark out the pattern of cuts. It's all very easy—if you have doubts, then just play around with a pair of compasses.*

Beginner's Workout

Although at first sight chip-carved designs do look to be complex, if you take a close-up look at a whole range of carvings, you will see that, in essence, the designs are made up from only three kinds of chip or slice cut. There is the incised cut that produces a three-cut V-section incised line; the three-cut triangular chip that leaves a little angled pocket; and the six-cut triangular chip that results in a little upturned, three-sided pyramid. If you can make these three chips, then all the other variations will follow.

Work on a strong bench or table, with your carving supported on a bench hook so that it can easily be turned and repositioned.

Making the Incised-Line Cut

Having studied this chapter and selected a piece of straight-grained wood, take one of your long-bladed knives—maybe the sheepsfoot—and get ready for action. Don't worry if you are a beginner—if your knife is sharp, and you are working on a stable surface, then you won't have problems. Keep in mind that as the three long cuts move variously with and across the grain, you will have to change the direction of the cuts to suit (see **4–11**).

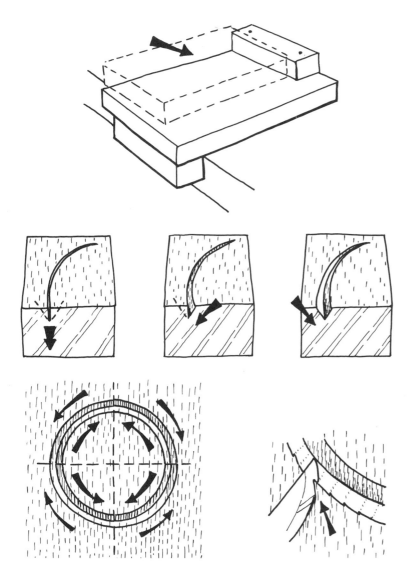

4–11 Chip-carving workout—making an incised cut with a knife. (Top) Having chosen a piece of prepared, knot-free, straight-grained, easy-to-carve wood, butt it hard up against the bench hook, and make sure that everything is stable and secure. (Middle—left to right) Once you have drawn in the shape and position of the trench, take a sharp knife and cut-sink a deep, straight-down stop-cut along the spine of the trench. It is best if this cut is achieved with a single stroke. When the initial stop-cut has been made—in the right position and to the required depth—make two follow-up and angled cuts—one at each side of the stop-cut. (Bottom left) If you want to cut an incised circle, then follow the same procedure already described, only this time keep changing the direction of the cut to follow the run of the grain. The arrows show the direction of the cuts; notice that cuts always avoid running into end grain. (Bottom right) If you cut in the wrong direction, the blade will run into the end grain and split the wood and/or result in a ragged cut. If you are a beginner, draw out various shapes on the wood—you could try your initials—and then play around with the knife until you have mastered the technique. Go for an easy-to-carve wood like linden/lime, basswood, or holly.

Making the Three-Cut Chip

Although the three-cut chip or pocket is made up from two down-stabbing cuts and a single wood-removing slicing cut, you will see that it is possible to increase the shape and form of the pocket by placing the pockets side by side (see **4–12**). This is how you develop the pattern.

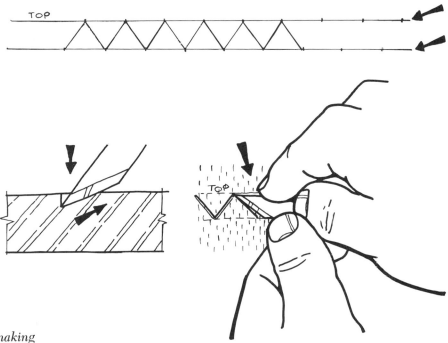

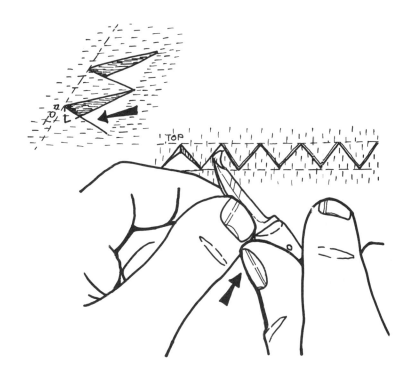

4–12 *Chip-carving workout—making the three-cut triangular chip. (Top) Having selected a piece of prepared easy-to-carve wood and made sure that your knife is good and sharp, use a pencil and ruler to set out the design. Have the lines parallel to each other and set at right angles across the run of the grain. Note how we have labelled one line "top." (Middle—left and right) With the zigzag line in place, take your knife and set it in with a series of straight-down stabbing cuts. Push the point of the knife in at the top of each zigzag—on the "top" line—and draw it towards you. Work with a steady dragging stroke. If you are doing it right, the deepest part of the cut will be on the "top" line. (Bottom—left and right) With the stop-cuts in place, take your knife— hold it so that the edge is facing the "top" line—and then remove each chip with a steady pushing-away-from-you stroke. If you have done it correctly, the chip pocket will have three faces—two vertical sides, and one as a sloping base.*

Making the Six-Cut Chip

Of all the cuts or motifs used in European chip carving, the six-cut chip is by far the most widely used. When you look at traditional designs, you will see that it is the placing of the six-cut pocket that primarily goes to make up the total design.

Note how the six-cut pocket is made up from three down-stabbing cuts that run out from the center of the triangle to the points and three angled slicing cuts that run from the sides of the triangle to the initial stabbing cuts (see **4–13**).

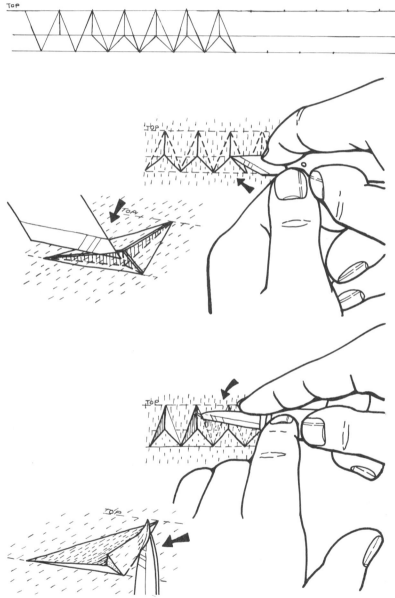

4–13 *Chip-carving workout—making the six-cut triangular chip. (Top) Set your wood out as before—with parallel lines and a zigzag—only this time around have three lines and divide each of the bottom triangles up into three smaller triangles, as shown—meaning the triangles that point towards the "top" line. (Middle—left and right) Stab in the stop-cuts in much the same way as already described, only this time position the cuts on the middle of the three parallel lines. The working procedure is to stab in deep at the center of the triangle and then to drag the blade out towards the point. (Bottom—left and right) With the stabbed stop-cuts in place, remove the waste with three angled slicing cuts. Make sure that cuts start on the sides of the zigzag. If you have it right, the pocket will have three angled faces. If you find that the wood is cutting up rough, then the wood may be unsuitable, perhaps damp, or the knife needs sharpening.*

Chapter 5

RELIEF AND PIERCED CARVING

Relief and pierced carving can be thought of as the next steps on from chip carving and incised work. As we imagine it, the craft of woodcarving must have evolved in a developmental way as a series of such steps, with the carver seeking to make deeper and more complex cuts. If the first tools were the axe, adze, and knife, then the corresponding first step in the evolutionary sequence of techniques had to do with converting trees into timber and timber into primary forms. Incised work and chip carving can be seen as the logical next steps: scratching about on the surface of the primary forms. Then it follows that relief work was another stride forward, leading naturally to pierced work as the inevitable result of working deeper and deeper.

Relief carving is, in essence, a technique that involves digging into the wood. The woodcarver works through stages of drawing out the design, setting it in with a V-section trench—much the same as with incised carving—making decisions as to the levels, and then setting to work lowering the various areas of waste. Generally speaking, relief carvings are only meant to be viewed from the front.

The skill of relief carving lies in being able to lower the waste ground and model the high-relief plateau in such a way that the two levels come together to make a convincing whole (see **5–1**). The terms *low* and *high* obviously describe the depth of the cuts and the resultant levels of the carved forms; but more than that, they are also terms that describe the degree and style of the carving. Although there is some confusion and crossover as to the meaning of the two terms— low relief sometimes also being called *deep*

relief—low relief is best defined as being an incised line design that has been partially lowered, whereas high relief is a design in which not only has part of the design been left standing proud—like an island in an ocean—but more than that, the "island" has been cut away and modelled—meaning shaped—so that it has three-dimensional form.

5–1 (Top left) Panel from an American "Sunflower" chest dated 1680. Note how the design is made up from two stylized motifs—the sunflower and the tulip. See also how the lowered ground has been punched. (Right) Detail from a four-poster bed— seventeenth century. (Bottom left) Elizabethan detail showing a slightly uncharacteristic strapwork motif.

To review, let's stay with the sea and land analogy. With low-relief carving describing a procedure where the ocean and the island are both equal flat-faced partners in the design (refer to **5–1**)—the sea simply being stepped down—then in high-relief carving not only is the ocean lower than the island, but both are contoured—or we would say modelled (see **5–2**). For example, if we were to carve foliage in low relief, it would first be incised, and then the surrounding area would be lowered. If we were to carve the same foliage in high relief, then once the ground area had been lowered, we would go on to model either the leaf and/or the surrounding ground.

If we push relief carving to the limits of the technique, we have a situation where just about all surfaces are relatively deeply carved, and maybe even undercut, with, perhaps, additional

5–2 *Deep relief work. (Top) Detail from the stern decoration on the schooner* Amphion, *built by F. H. Chapman in 1779. Painted blue and gilt. The face is naturalistically carved in deep relief (Statens Sjöhistoriska Museum, Venice, Italy). (Middle) Ship's stern decoration—eighteenth century. Carved in deep relief with a good amount of undercutting (National Scheepraart Museum, Steen, Netherlands). (Bottom) Carved and painted detail from ship's stern board—from a theme entitled "Solomon's Ordeal." Deeply carved and undercut (Groningen, Netherlands).*

5–3 *Built-up and applied work, carved in linden/ lime wood by Edmund Carpenter in the tradition of Grinling Gibbons. An account dated 1688 declares that Sir John Brownlow paid Edmund Carpenter 25 pounds sterling for his work. (Belton House, Lincolnshire, England) Although this piece is described as being carved from a single piece of wood, it's plain to see on close inspection that in part there are pegged and glued additions and extensions. Our feeling is, however, that these are original.*

elements glued on and then carved (see **5–3**).

If we push relief carving beyond its limits, we create pierced carving, where the lowered ground areas have pierced the wood to become windows (see **5–4**).

Having accepted that the many relief carving terms and definitions have to do with the amount of wood that is cut away—meaning the depth, the amount of undercutting, the shape, the size and proportion of the wood left standing in relief, and the amount of linkage between the carved area and the ground wood—then it's important to note that relief carving is such a huge, worldwide, multifaceted subject that separate areas have, over the years, been given names that cloud the fact that they are simply relief carvings.

5–4   Pierced and carved oak pew ends—front and back views—Dutch, sixteenth century. Note the drilled pattern of holes. (Victoria and Albert Museum, London)

Relief carvings include architectural panels termed *linenfolds*; repeat patterns termed *gouge-carved mouldings*; stylized patterns termed *Jacobean strapwork*; naturalistic interpretations of birds, flowers and figures; polyglot panels that show abstracted imagery; name boards with lettering cut away and/or raised in relief; stylized religious images and patterns on church furniture and interiors; designs carved on forms that have already been turned and/or carved in the round; and so on.

Such carvings do look quite different one from another, which may confuse beginners, and yet they are all examples of relief carving. The defining factors that unite all these branches and offshoots as being relief carving are the choice of tools, the techniques used to remove the wood, and the degree and depth of carving.

If you are a beginner and still confused, then our best advice is to press on, studying our descriptions of tools and tool usage, and then try one or all of the exercises.

Tools and Usage

We suspect that many prospective beginners to woodcarving are scared away simply by seeing the imponderable array of tools shown in most catalogs; there are hundreds of different types (see 5–5), all with fancy names, and all described as being the one-and-only, best-ever tool for such and such a task. We do agree reservedly with the old woodcarving adage that says that a huge tool kit will not make a good carver, but, that said, we think that by the time you reach the stage when you want to try your hand at relief work, then, to a great extent, your success will depend on your tools as well as the way that you use them. A good part of the technique of relief carving involves using the correct tool for the task. But then again, if you are a raw beginner, we can't know your specific area of interest, and you can't be expected to rush out and purchase a whole heap of tools. What to do?

To help you make well-informed decisions, we will concentrate on presenting the sequence of cuts that go to make up a typical relief carving, specific difficult-to-do procedures, and the general techniques of holding and using the tools. The hands-on illustrations and descriptions cover all manner of relief carving situations and procedures, but they are set out in what might be described as a first-to-last sequence. With just about any relief carving, you would set the design in with an incised line, then chop the line in with such and such a tool, and lower the ground, and so on.

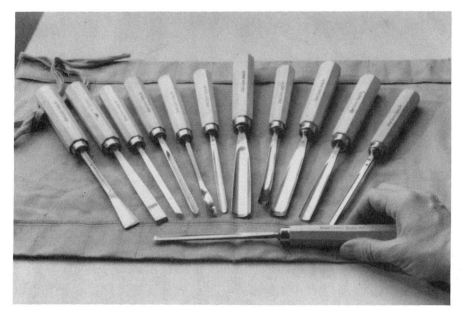

5–5 *A set of Lamp brand tools. Not only have the twelve tools been carefully selected with the beginner in mind, but better yet, they are honed and ready to use. This last point is worth bearing in mind, because many tools are sold in the need-to-be-honed state— not a good idea for beginners.*

Outlining or Wasting

When the design has been fully considered, sequentially drawn out to full size on a sheet of workout paper, traced, and pencil-press transferred to the surface of the wood that is to be carved, then the area that is to be left in relief needs to be outlined, and the resultant ground lowered. This procedure is termed, variously, wasting the ground, outlining, or lowering the waste ground; different communities or regions use different terms.

There are at least four ways that this procedure can be managed—it's your preference. You could (1) set-in the drawn line with a straight-down stop-cut, and then skim out the waste with one or another of the bent, spoon, or dog-leg tools; (2) cut a V-section trench slightly to the waste side of the drawn line, and then set-in the drawn line with a straight-down stop-cut before skimming out the ground (see **5–6**); (3) cut the V-trench to the waste side of the drawn line, and then skim off the waste

ground before setting-in the drawn line; or (4) lower the bulk of the ground with one or another of the skimming tools, and then tidy up the drawn line with a straight-down cut.

Although all four of these techniques are valid, traditionally acceptable, and will get the job done, the first technique—meaning to chop the drawn line in with a straight-down stop-cut, and then to lower the waste—is a little suspect, in that sometimes the force of the straight-down chopping action is enough to split and do damage to the slender areas of the design. And then again, the fourth method—simply skimming out the bulk of the waste ground before setting-in the outline—sometimes results in the tool overrunning the drawn line and doing damage to the area that you want to leave in relief. We prefer the approach of the middle two methods—first outlining with a V-tool before setting-in and then wasting, or vice versa—for two reasons (see **5–6** and **5–7**). First, when the setting-in procedure is underway, the V-trench diverts the damaging wedge-like action of the tool, in as much as the side of the V-trench crumbles away rather than the design. Second, when the waste is being skimmed away, the V-trench acts as a stop-cut.

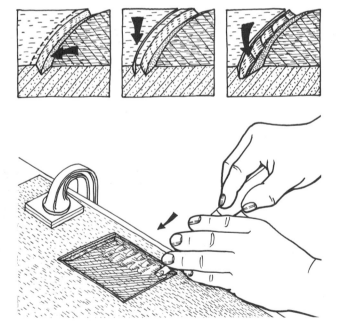

5–6 *Outlining and wasting. (Top—left to right) Cut a V-section trench a little to the waste side of the drawn line; sink the drawn line in with a stop-cut; clear out the waste between the stop-cut and the trench and then waste the ground. (Bottom) With the workpiece held securely in a clamp, use a straight gouge to swiftly clear the bulk of the waste.*

5–7 *When you come to lower the waste, work backwards—or we might say, retreat from a "cliff" edge—so that there is a minimum of resistance to your subsequent cutting strokes.*

As to how best to cut the V-trench—meaning the incised line—you can either use a knife or a small V-section tool or a veiner as in **5–8** and **5–9**. The choice of tool will to a great extent depend on the density of the wood, the scale of the carving, your strength, and your own way of working.

Wasting Away with a Drill

Having described traditional methods of outlining and wasting, it follows that there are less traditional alternatives when utilizing modern tools. One such alternative—best used when working on a deep relief that has a ground of uniform depth—is to swiftly waste the ground with a bench drill press or a hand drill before outlining. Although this method is beautifully simple and direct, you do, of course, need a drill and a set of Forstner bits.

The procedure—once you have set out the design as already described—is to shade in the ground, to set the drill to the required depth, and then simply to cover the ground area with a honeycomb of holes. If you work through the bit sizes from large to small, you will eventually reach a

point where just about all of the waste has been removed (see **5–10**).

Although this method is amazingly swift, it is wearing on the drill, on the bits, and on the nerves. Inevitably, the drill gets hot, the small-diameter bits tend to break, and the whole procedure is noisy and dusty. And one last word about using the drill: the entire operation only really works if you use good-quality Forstner bits—bits that are capable of boring out crisp, clean-sided, flat-bottomed holes—and a drill with a depth guide or stop.

Be Warned If you try to use flat bits or twist bits, then the sides of the carving will be rough and raggedy, the surface of the lowered ground will be marked by the point of the drill bit, and the whole operation will likely come to grief.

Setting-In

Once the overall design has been outlined with a V-section trench and the ground has been swiftly wasted—meaning lowered—then the part of the design that is to be left proud has to be set-in with a stop-cut. The function of the cut is to define the edge of the design and to control cuts made when

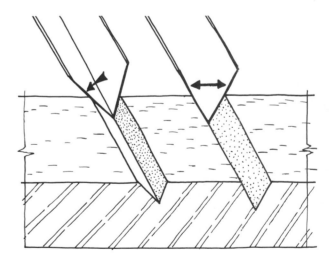

5–8 *When you are using the V-tool to outline the design, have one hand holding and the other pushing and guiding. Working in this way, one hand acts as a control, while the other does the work.*

5–9 *Using a V-tool for cutting incised lines makes a cut of uniform depth—generally no more than about ³⁄₁₆in (4.5mm). The point of the tool needs to be held upright so that the cutting forces are equally distributed. Make a series of short passes or cuts to work around a curve.*

5-10 *Using a power drill to clear the bulk of the lowered waste. We used three different-size Forstner bits for this project, with a strip of masking tape as a depth stop guide. This was a very hard piece of English oak—the smallest of the three bits broke in use.*

the ground is being cleaned up. The procedure involves taking various cutting tools that fit the curves—knives, gouges, or chisels—setting them vertically on the drawn line, and cutting straight down into the wood to the depth of the lowered ground (see **5-11**). Depending on the depth of the cut and/or the hardness of the wood, the tool can either be tapped in with a mallet or simply pushed.

Setting-in is pretty straightforward, as long as the cuts are all of a uniform depth, and as long as they all fit together to follow the drawn outline. The tool can be either held perfectly upright, so that the resultant "cliff" is at a right angle to the bed of the ground or canted back at a slight angle with the handle leaning over the design so that the "cliff" runs at a slope down from the design to the ground.

5-11 *To make a straight-down stabbing cut—working across the run of the grain— make a slight side-to-side rocking movement, while at the same time pushing hard down on the handle. With a larger workpiece you might have to put the weight of your chest and shoulders behind the thrust.*

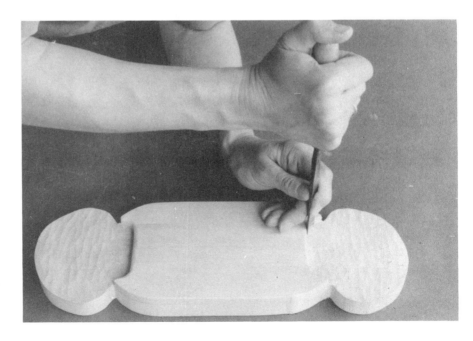

The choice of tools and the actual holds are both important factors that affect the finish. For example, if you take a straight chisel and belt it with a mallet—the wrong chisel and too hard a blow—then the wood might well split and/or crumble. Or then again, if you are a total beginner and are trying to set-in with a bent gouge or maybe a dogleg chisel, then the force of the thrust might well result in damage to the design and/or the tool.

Our best advice, if you are a beginner looking to set-in a piece of easy-to-carve wood, is to hold the tool so as to make a straight stabbing or thrusting stroke and to make a series of "false" or backing-up cuts. For example, if you are right-handed,

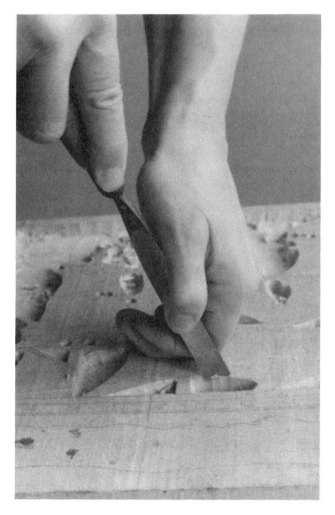

5–12   Steep-sided holes need to be cut at a slight skewing angle; push down on the handle with one hand and control and guide with the other hand.

hold the handle of your chosen straight chisel or gouge in your right hand—with the butt under your thumb or in your palm—set your thumb and index finger to either side of the blade, and then push the blade into the wood. As to the way your right hand grips the handle of the tool, the thumb on top of the handle is best for a cut that needs to be carefully placed (refer to **5–11**), whereas the palm-over-the-butt hold is best for a lighter, curved cut (see **5–12**).

Setting-in is a simple procedure, for which confidence and knowledge will come with practice; nevertheless, it is a procedure that requires judgment as to the best tool for the task. If the design is broadly curved and flowing, then there is no problem; your tools will more than likely fit the curves. But if the design is tight and made up of curves, then you will have to make the most of your gouge shapes or even use a knife.

Generally speaking, we tend to use small, flat curve tools and lots of strokes. From our experience, we've found that many small cuts with a small tool are less likely to do damage than a few big cuts with a big tool. If this doesn't make a lot of sense, then we suggest you have to go right away and draw out a complex curve on a slab of scrap wood to see what happens.

Grounding or Bosting

Once the design has been outlined and wasted, and set-in with a carefully placed line of stop-cuts, then comes the procedure known as grounding or

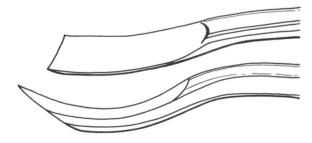

5–13   Skewed spoon gouges. These combine the spoon curvature that is helpful for getting into tight areas with the angled blade of the skew. A really good tool for shearing and skimming into tight or awkward areas of lowered ground.

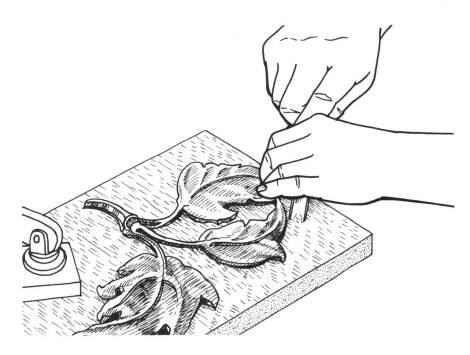

5–14 *Using a shallow-sweep gouge to lightly texture the background. In this instance, the motif has been fretted out, glued, pegged to a backboard, and then carved.*

bosting. A couple of fancy names maybe, but all these terms refer to is the procedure of skimming the waste ground around the design down to the required level and to a good finish (see **5–13** and **5–14**).

Although this is a pretty straightforward process of selecting one or other of the bent tools and simply running low skimming cuts across or at a slight angle to the grain to level the ground, we find that the kinds of mistake that most beginners make are to use the wrong tool and/or to try for a surface that is just too smooth. Beginners commonly make the error of using a bent tool with a chisel edge, in which case they scratch the ground, or of using a straight tool, in which case they can't reach all of the ground (see **5–15**).

5–15 *Grounding or bosting. (Top) The shallow-sweep, bent gouge enables you to ground out the waste without doing damage to the edges of areas left in relief and without digging the corners of the tool into the lowered ground. (Bottom) Using a straight chisel in this instance is a bad idea on several counts—the shaft does damage on the edges of the design; the corners of the blade tear the lowered ground; and the straight blade means that you can't easily reach all of the waste that needs to be removed.*

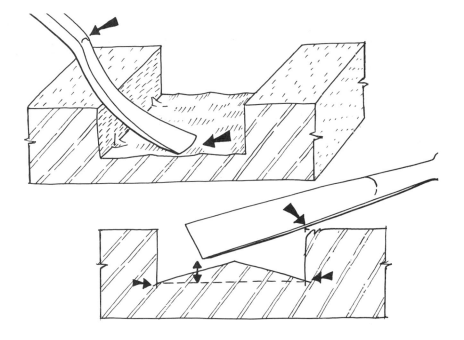

It's all beautifully uncomplicated, and you won't go far wrong if you stay with a couple of rules of thumb: the ground has to be clean and smooth, but not so smooth that it looks machined;

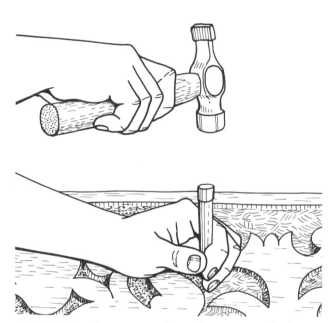

5–16 *Using hammer and punch to texture the lowered ground. Have the workpiece well supported on a bed of newspapers or old rags—to minimize the risk of the wood splitting and to cut down the noise.*

the bent tool has to have a shallow-sweep cutting edge that is just curved enough to lift the corners of the blade clear of the ground. As to the type of finish, you have to make the decision whether you want the ground to be textured with lots of dappled scoops. If you do, then you need to use a wide shallow-sweep tool. If you'd rather that the texture show a more pecked effect, then you need to use a smaller U-section blade.

Finally, having said that the ground needs to be level and crisply worked, if your work is, perhaps, less than perfect—a mess even—then you might decide to go for a cover-up punched texture. Although punching would seem to us too easy a way out for our work, it is a good way of bringing the ground to an overall uniform texture. All you do is take the punch of your choice—there are many pattern designs to choose from—and systematically go over the ground, tapping in the texture (see **5–16**).

Modelling

Once the more mechanical procedures are out of the way—the setting-in, the grounding, and all the rest—then comes the exciting task of modelling—meaning the process of shaping. If

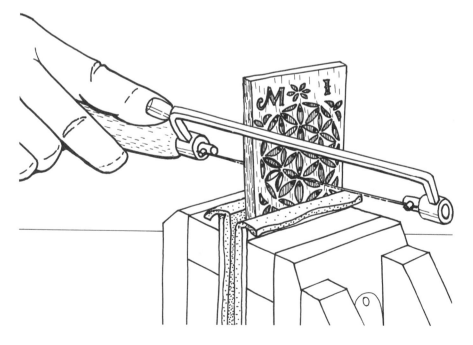

5–17 *To pierce a window, drill a guide or pilot hole through the waste that needs to be cut away, pass the blade of the saw through the hole, hitch up the blade and retension, and then set to work cutting out the window. Use a muffled vise to hold the workpiece, and have the area being worked positioned well down near the vise.*

you simply want to go for a stylized strapwork-type design, all you do is skim off the surface of the design—in much the same way as you did for the ground—and the job is done. However, with most relief carvings, modelling is the stage when the carver can really experiment with textures, depths of cut, and form, and with all the other personal judgments that go to make a good carving. (Refer to Chapter 6 on sculptural carving for specific tool holds.)

Piercing

Piercing is no more or less than a term used to describe a carving—it can be relief carved or sculptural—that is in some way or other pierced with holes or windows. In the context of relief carving, the pierced holes tend to be either an extension of high-relief work, in which case the lowered ground areas are so deep that they pierce the wood—as in various Gothic church traceries and furniture carving—or holes and windows cut through thin boards—as with a good many folk art carvings (see **5–17**). With regard to techniques, holes can, of course, be chopped through with gouges, pierced with a drill, or fretted with one or other of the saws—it depends on the context.

Primary Tools and Proper Handling Techniques

If you want to be free to go your own way and really enjoy woodcarving, then you do need to be able to use the various tools with confidence. You need to know the many ways that a tool can be held, the most efficient ways of working, and all the other little tricks of the trade. The following batch of handling techniques and tips will get you started.

Mallet Cuts

If you are working on a good-size carving, and you want to clear away a lot of waste fast, then you

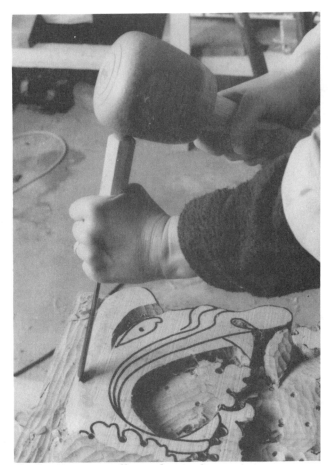

5–18 Using a mallet and straight gouge to cut across end grain. Working on this English oak—a hard, knotty, and damp piece—we cut at a sloping angle to the grain, all the while make a swift series of small cuts.

can't do better than use a mallet and a sharp gouge. However, a mistake that most beginners make is that they overdo; they take the biggest gouge and the heaviest mallet, and then set to work in deadly earnest trying to clear great chunks of waste. And, of course, what usually happens is that the tool gets stuck, their arms get tired, and they generally finish up by variously splitting the wood, damaging the tool, or having a dangerous shop accident.

With the mallet held loosely, you need to do the work with little swift movements—lots of light, low-angled, lively blows—all the time being ready, to re-angle the tool, and/or move the wood to approach the grain to best effect (see **5–18**).

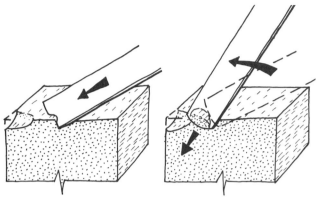

5–19 *Modelling end grain. Take only small cuts, with the blade moving at a low, skewed slicing angle.*

Straight-and-Strong Cuts

A good part of the time, woodcarving is achieved with what we call the straight-and-strong cut. All this means is that the carver takes a straight gouge, holds it in one hand so that the butt end of the handle is in the palm, supports and guides the stroke with the other hand, and then puts the full weight and strength of the carver's shoulders behind the stroke. Working in this way, we find that not only can we cut through the toughest wood with the minimum of effort, but better yet, we can be pretty certain that the cut is fully controlled (see **5–19**, **5–20**, **5–21**, and **5–22**).

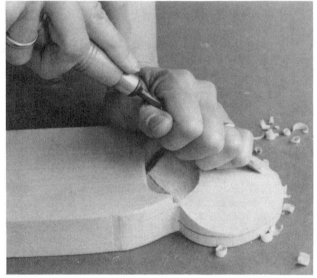

5–20 *To cut a sloping plain in soft wood, push forward with a tight, controlled grasping stroke. In this context, we tended to skim the blade with a shearing stroke.*

5–21 *Lowering a level plain. Working across the run of the grain, push at a low, slicing skimming angle. If the grain is difficult, then work with a slight rocking action. Aim all the while for a slightly dappled, tooled finish.*

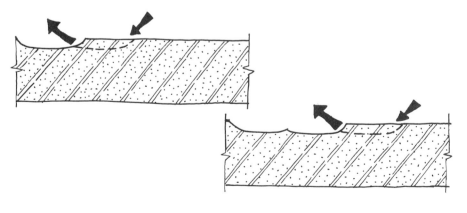

5–22 *Lowering a level plain. Working with a shallow-sweep gouge and small overlapping strokes, the carver retreats across the workpiece. (Left) The second stroke overlaps the first. (Right) The overlapping and retreating action swiftly lowers the waste. The small peaks are removed on a second pass.*

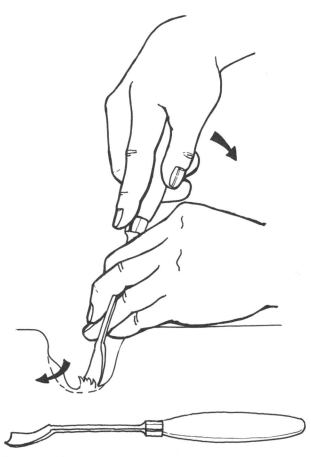

5–23 *Using a spoon or bent gouge to carve a hollow. The tool is held and pivoted down low near the blade with one hand, and worked with a small paddling action by the other hand. The movement results in an efficient cut.*

Using the Spoon Gouge

The spoon or bent gouge is a great tool for scooping out deep reliefs and hollows. The way the tool is held and maneuvered greatly affects its efficiency. We tend to use two cuts—the scooping cut and the hold-down cut.

The scooping cut is self-explanatory—it's just like using a spoon for scooping out a hard-boiled egg or ice cream. In use, the tool is held with the butt of the handle pressed into the palm of the hand and with the index finger of the same hand pointing down the shaft. The maneuver is controlled with a light three-finger hold by the other hand. With the butt-gripping hand doing the work, and with the fingers of the other hand being the fulcrum, the tool is lightly seesawed and twisted (see **5–23**).

The hold-down cut is best used when you are working on a deep relief—when you want to remove a relatively large amount of wood. In use, although the tool is held in much the same way as the scooping out—that is, with one hand around the handle and the other around the shaft—both hands are put to work in a much heavier, more forceful way. The holding hand supplies the thrust and push, while the other hand presses and pushes down on the shaft. The end result of this way of working is that the tool cuts long and deep, the left hand preventing the blade from exiting before the cut is complete (see **5–24**).

5–24 *Using the spoon gouge to cut a deep and sudden curve—on a deep relief or a sculptural carving, for example—the blade is thrust in with one hand, while the handle is levered back with the other. The down-pressure of the levelling hand prevents the blade from exiting before the cut is complete.*

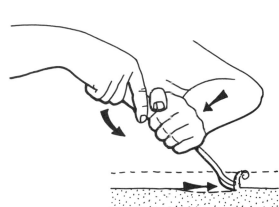

Down-Chopping with the Gouge

The down-chopping cut is best used where you want to make a single, strong, well-placed stroke. In use, the tool is held with both hands grasping and with the thumbs of both hands looking skyward. The grasping hands to the work, while the thumbs act as a guide to the vertical straightness of the cut (see **5–25**).

Using the Veiner Tool

Although we don't use a veiner tool very much—because we are really more at home with a knife—there are times when the veiner is maybe the best tool for the task (see **5–26**). Although it is in many ways a wonderfully easy-to-use tool, we find that it has a tendency to run into the grain. In use, the veiner is held with the butt of the handle tucked into the palm of the hand—so that the index finger points the way—and with the fingers of the other hand guiding and controlling the cut. By putting the weight of your shoulder behind the thrust, it is possible to cut even the hardest of woods.

Knife Cuts

We are very fond of using a knife—so much so, that we probably use it when another tool may get the job done faster. But why make excuses—a woodcarver is most comfortable using a particular tool, and if it gets the job done, then why not stay with it?

The knife can be used for making V-cuts and stop-cuts, for skimming, and for shaving convex surfaces, and so on—it's a good all-around tool. To our way of thinking, the knife is a really good tool for setting-in stop-cuts around small curves—as in the eyes of the lion shown in **5–27**.

Using Bent Tools

Bent tools are great for getting into corners and crevices that would otherwise be inaccessible. In the instance shown in **5–28**, a slightly skewed, shallow-curve, dog-leg-type gouge is used for cleaning up the difficult-to-reach corner. Our best advice, if you are just starting out, is to get a small,

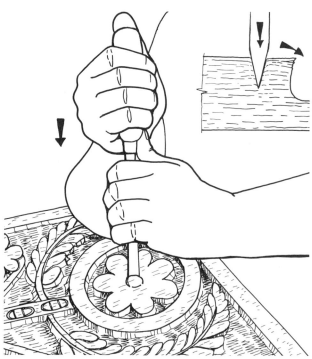

5–25 *Down-chopping cut. (Left) When working on a soft easy-to-carve wood, the down-chopping cut can be achieved with a two-handed thrust. (Right) Be warned—if you want to make a cut alongside an area that has already been lowered, then do not push a tool in as shown. If you do, then the edge is liable to crumble. In this instance, you would use a knife or V-tool to cut a trench, before making the down-thrusting cut.*

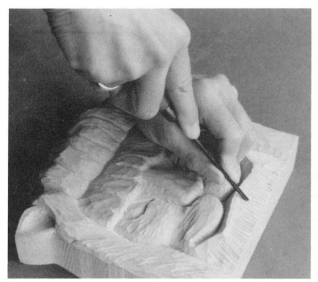

5–26 *Using a veiner tool. The veiner should never be rolled or twisted, but rather the trench is best cut with an overlapping series of scoops.*

narrow-width bent tool—one with a very shallow, almost flat curve. We say this, because such a tool can be used for most tasks. And, of course, if you are working on a big carving, one with large corners and angles, then it won't much matter anyway, since you will be able to use all manner of other tools for cleaning out the waste.

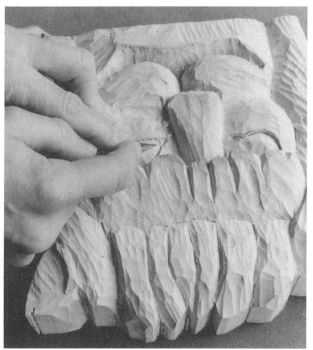

5–27 *Using a knife to tidy up the small details. We favor using small, sharp penknives for detail work on soft wood.*

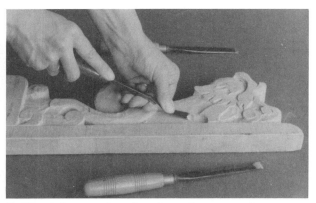

5–28 *A bent tool with a skewed cutting edge is really good for cleaning out small corners and angles.*

Beginner's Workout

Although relief carving is a broad subject, there being all manner of offshoots, if we pare the technique down to its essentials, there are four basic stages: lining the design in with a V-cut and wasting; setting-in and grounding; modelling; and piercing holes. If you can sort out these four technique stages, then all the rest is up to good old-fashioned practice.

Cutting V-Trenches and Wasting

After you have read through this chapter, then select a piece of straight-grained, easy-to-carve wood, take a small, straight V-tool, a couple of small-width, shallow-sweep straight gouges, and a mallet, and have a tryout. It is best if you are working on a strong, stable bench or table with the workpiece held securely down by a clamp or holdfast (see **5–29**).

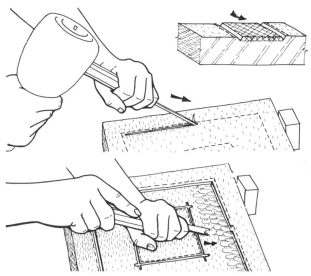

5–29 *Cutting V-trenches and wasting. (Top and middle) Having drawn out the lines of the design, take a mallet and a V-tool, and cut V-section trenches a little to the waste side of the drawn line. (Bottom) With the trenches in place, use a straight gouge to lower the waste. Note how this order of working—the V-trench cut before the straight-down stop-cut—results very neatly in the small angle of waste wood between the lowered ground and the drawn line, acting as a buffer or fender to take any wasting cuts that overrun.*

Setting-In and Grounding

Having worked through the previous exercise, take another piece of wood—or you might use the same piece—a mallet, a selection of small-width straight gouges, and a couple of bent gouges, secure the wood to the bench and work through the setting-in and grounding procedures. Don't worry at this stage about trying to carve an actual design or motif, just concentrate your efforts on achieving clean lines and a level ground—both with the minimum of ragged tool marks (see 5–30).

Modelling

This is the technique stage that separates the truly skilled from the unskilled. We admit that you can't expect to master the art of relief carving over-night, but you can at least give it your best shot.

You need a piece of wood that has been taken through the two previous procedures and a selection of razor-sharp tools. The secret is to take your time, and to work with or at an angle to, not against, the grain. If you can figure out how to keep the tools sharp, and how to use the grain to best advantage, then you are well on your way to being a carver (see 5–31).

Piercing a Hole

Piercing is easy; all you need is a thin piece of wood, a drill with a small-diameter bit—about ¼in (6mm)—a coping saw, the use of a bench fitted with a vise, and a pack of spare saw blades (see 5–32).

Note: You might also use a power scroll saw and an electric drill.

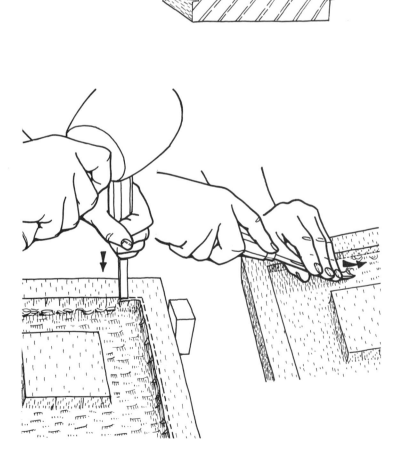

5–30 Setting-in and grounding. (Top) Having cut a V-section trench to the waste side of the drawn line and swiftly wasted—meaning cleared the bulk of waste from the area around the design—you should be left with a situation where the ground still needs to be skimmed slightly lower, and the small strip of waste between the drawn line and the ground needs to be cut out or set-in with a stop-cut. (Left) When you are ready to set-in the drawn line, take a straight tool—a chisel for a straight line, or one or other of the gouges to fit a curved line; set the cutting edge down on the line so that the tool is vertical; and give it a sharp, lively tap with the mallet. Work around the drawn line, all the while setting-in a linked chain of stop-cuts down to the required depth. Although it's a fairly easy procedure, you do have to make sure that the handle of the tool is either directly upright or slightly angled over the high-relief area. On no account must the "cliff" face be undercut. If you are doing it correctly, most of the strip of waste will crumble away from the drawn line. (Right) With the drawn line crisply set-in with a stop-cut, use a shallow-sweep bent tool to skim the ground to a smooth, tooled finish.

5–31 *Modelling. Having skimmed off the ground and achieved a nice, clean and crisp "cliff" edge, then comes the not-so-easy task of modelling. If your tools are sharp, you pay attention to the direction of the grain, and you make sure that all your cuts are small and well placed, then at least you won't be battling against the odds. Be mindful that this exercise contains a whole mess of tricky problem cuts. (Top right) Having decided on the shape of the area that you want to model and shaded in the area that needs to be worked, have a look at the run of the grain, and then plan the direction of the cuts to fit. (Top left) To round-over the outer edge of the dome, work either with or at an angle to the grain—so that the tool cuts from high to low wood. (Bottom right) Once you have modelled the outer edge of the dome, take a smaller tool, and lower the inner moat that runs around the central bump. This little stage is particularly tricky in that the moat runs in a circle over the direction of the grain. (Bottom left) This detail shows the overall direction of the cuts needed to model the bump.*

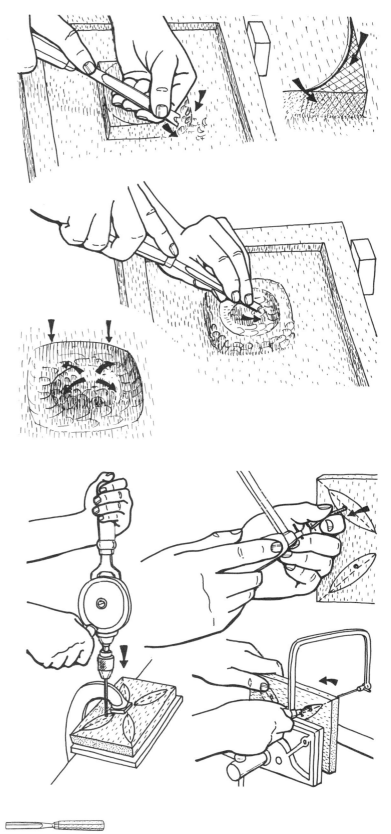

5–32 *Piercing a hole. (Left) Having carefully marked in the windows that need to be cut away, set the workpiece over a waster—meaning a piece of scrap wood—and drill a pilot hole through each window of waste. The size of the hole isn't critical, as long as it's big enough to take the saw blade but not so big that it touches the drawn lines. (Top right) Pass the saw blade through the hole, rehitch, and retension. The teeth need to be facing towards the handle, and the blade must ping when plucked. (Bottom) With the wood held secure in the vise so that the area to be worked is close to the jaws, cut out the waste. Repeat this procedure for all of the windows. It's not difficult as long as the blade is sharp and well tensioned, the blade is always presented in line with the next cut, and the line of cut is slightly to the waste side of the drawn line.*

Chapter 6

SCULPTURAL CARVING

Certainly sculptural—also called carving in the round—is the next step, in terms of technique, on from relief carving, with the carver cutting deeper and deeper until the imagery can be viewed from all angles. But it is really a rather radical departure in terms of concept and approach. Or to put it another way, whereas we primarily think of relief carving as being a decorative procedure that has to do with embellishing flat surfaces, most of us see sculptural carving as being a somewhat magical art form that engages the eyes and mind into believing that the carving has life.

We would say that wood sculpture, or carving in the round, has to do with interpreting nature in terms of wood—although some would take issue with such a broad generalization. A carver might set out to sculpt an apple, for example, all the while trying to create an object that is, as far as possible, real. The sculptor will be trying to do his or her level best to make us believe that the carved apple is something that you can pick up and view from many angles—an apple that is almost good enough to eat, and complete with details and imperfections such as worm holes, a stem, and a couple of leaves.

The exciting thing is that no two carvers will see the apple in the same way. For example, one sculptor might carve a bird that is a life-like copy of nature, whereas another sculptor might interpret a bird as being more stylized, and another sculptor might see the bird as some smooth, abstracted form. And one sculptor's work might in some way or other just be inspired by birds and the idea of flight, without there being a recognizable bird anywhere.

Although the woodcarver who works in the round generally uses the same tools, techniques, and materials as the relief carver, the philosophy

6–1 The grid is a swift and easy way of taking measurements and making enlargements. For example, if we take it that the scale of this drawing is one square to one inch, then just by counting the squares, we can see that the figure stands 36 inches (91cm) high and 24 inches (61cm) wide across the span of the war bonnet.

and conceptual approach is completely different. To our way of thinking, sculptural carving involves a bigger, more expansive, more dynamic approach.

As always, if you are a beginner, then our best advice is to study our descriptions here of tools and tool usage and then brush up your skills by trying one or all of the workout exercises.

Tools and Usage

Although sculptural carving techniques are much the same as those used in relief carving—with the carver working in sequence through the various stages of designing, setting-in, wasting, lowering, and modelling—sculptural carving differs and is made more complicated by the fact that these activities are carried out, at one and the same time, on all faces of the wood. To us, sculptural carving procedures seem more intense, there being a need for a lot of planning ahead before any tool is put to the wood.

The following sequence of technique events and hands-on tools situations—taken from a whole range of different woodcarving projects—will give you an idea of how we work, of all the stages we travel through from the initial idea, or commission, to handing over the sculpture.

Research and Gridded Working Drawings

When we have been given a commission—let's say to carve a Native American figure, or maybe a lion—we usually start by raking around through our collection of books, old magazines, and photographs just to see what we have on the subject. We then follow this up by visiting the library and city museums, asking friends and neighbors, and generally doing our best to gather as much relevant information as possible. If the subject is an animal, then we might take a trip to the nearest zoo. We feel that the more that we know about our subject, then the better our project is going to pan out. We think of the research as being a fun time, a time of exploration and discovery.

At home, we assemble all our finds, clip photos from magazines, and generally spend time pinning the material up on the walls. This done, we sit back and decide, in the light of our findings, the time available, our stock of wood, and our tool kit, just how the project needs to go. Having made decisions as to size and stance, we then get down to the task of making sketches and drawings. Between the two of us, Gillian usually sketches out as many views as possible—front, side, back, and top—then hands the sketches over to Alan so that he can make working drawings. Be warned that this process usually involves lots of heated discussions and crumpled-up bits of paper before we get it right. Finally, we draw the sketches out on gridded and scaled sheets of paper (see 6–1 and 6–2) and make full-size copies and tracings. Depending on the size of the work, we sometimes speed up this end procedure by making photocopies. The general idea is that we have a set of master drawings that we keep clean—to be filed away for future reference—and a set of copies that go to the workshop that usually end up being cut and torn.

6–2 Front and side views of a lion's head. We made a drawing of this character before we made a maquette.

Building a Maquette

With all the working drawings to size, having taken tracings, and hammered together a support or armature from bits and pieces of wood, wire, and nails, we take our tracings, Plasticine, and modelling equipment to a little corner that we have set aside in the kitchen—it's warm with plenty of light—and set to work on the painstaking task of building a maquette, that is to say, a working model (see **6–3**). It is best if the maquette is full-size, but if this isn't possible, we start by building a scaled-down model of the whole image, and then build particular details at full sculptural size. For example, with the fairground horse shown in **6–3**, we first built it at about quarter scale, and then made full-size details of the parts that we thought were going to be tricky. At the end of the procedure, we had the maquette of the whole head and a macabre little collection of bits—an eye in a socket, an ear, a nostril, and part of the lip.

The modelling procedure usually involves us in working with dividers, callipers, a tape measure, matchsticks, bits of string, strips of paper, and anything else that helps us to transfer measurements and step-offs from the tracings to the Plasticine.

Laminating and Working on the Band Saw

Having completed the maquette, we move to the workshop, and set the model and the drawings up so that they are within view but out of harm's way. This done, we make more-detailed decisions as to how the carving is going to "come out" of the wood. No problem if it's a little miniature—we can usually find a bit of wood that fits—but if the project is big, then we have to decide how we are going to build up and laminate the wood to make a composite form. If we are working in a soft wood that's going to be painted, as in, say, a figurehead

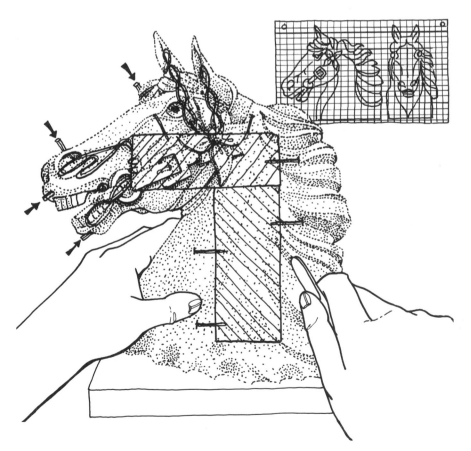

6–3 *Having made the working drawing, build a wire and wood armature to support the weight of the Plasticine, and then set to work building the maquette. We use matchsticks to mark the main reference points, and callipers and dividers to transfer the measurement step-offs.*

or cigar store figure, then we use 4in (10.2cm) square sections, and stack them together to make the block. Or then again, if we are working on a figure that has its arm set out away from the body or a decoy duck that has a head set into the body, we would search around for pieces and types of wood that fit. With work that is going to be painted, we find that it's a good idea to build the block up from lots of small sections. The idea is that not only can a lot of the roughing out be done on the band saw, but, better yet, a form that is built up from lots of small sections—with the grain generally running along the length of the details—is less likely to distort and crack when it's drying out.

Having decided how the wood is going to be blocked up, we do our best to pencil-press transfer the imagery to at least one side of the wood. What usually happens is that we wind up cutting the tracings into small pieces to fit the various sides and planes of the wood. This stage isn't easy, because all the time we are trying to, as it were,

"see" what is "happening" inside the wood.

When we have transferred the imagery, shaded in the waste areas, and pencil-labelled all the bits so that we know what goes where and how, we then move to the band saw and set to work cutting out the various profiles (see **6–4**). Wherever possible, we fret the image out, as seen in one view, set the bits of waste back in place so that we can see the drawn imagery on the other face, and then fret the image as seen in the other view. Of course, this procedure only works if you are working with prepared wood, and it takes a lot of figuring out, but if you can manage it, then it saves a lot of sweat and toil at a later stage. We find that it's all pretty straightforward as long as we pencil-label all the bits and pieces as soon as they are cut.

Knowing that most of our carvings end up painted, we can use a small amount of filler to make good. If you are working on a carving where you want all the grain on view, then you have to spend a lot of time making sure that all the faces that are to be glued come together for a good fit.

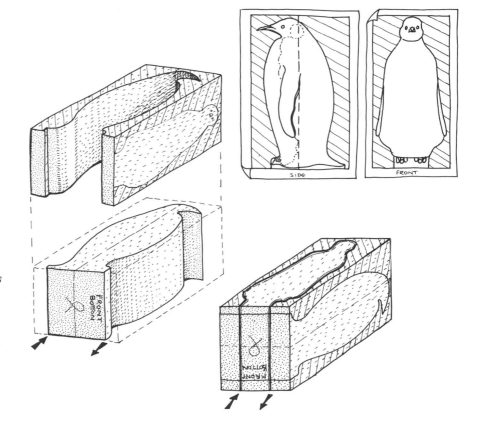

6–4 Having drawn the views of the design at full size, made tracing, pencil-press transferred the traced lines to the wood, and labelled the various sides and faces, then cut out the profile as seen in one view, reassemble the pieces, and then cut the profile out as seen in the other view. We use this system even when we are building a large carving from lots of laminated parts.

Gluing and Clamping Up

Once a good deal of the waste has been cleared on the band saw, then comes the fun-filled, tricky, sticky task of gluing and clamping up. First and foremost, you need to clear the workshop of clutter, and plan the whole exercise like a military campaign. Working surfaces have to be cleared, the wood must be set out in order, the glue must be prepared, the clamping system must be sorted, and generally, you must have a clear picture in your mind's eye as to the order of work. What we usually do is have a practice dry run—we find that it helps us to sort out potential problems.

When everything is ready to go, and after first sprinkling a small amount of sawdust over the floor of our workshop to soak up excess glue, we smear a generous amount of glue on mating faces, bring the various elements together, and then clamp up.

As to the type of clamps that we use, much depends on the size and shape of the component parts. If, for example, we are just bringing two flat-faced blocks together, we might use a single-sash-type window bar clamp (see **6–5**), or then again, if we are dealing with a bundle of partly sawn components, as in, say, a laminated fig-urehead (see **6–6**), then we might use a rope binding and wedges—it all depends. Finally, we sweep up the sawdust and generally clear away all the throwaway containers, sticks, and brushes that we have used for gluing.

Roughing Out

Once the glue has set, and the clamps and/or bindings and wedges have been removed, then comes the stage known as roughing out—meaning clearing away the bulk of the waste. We usually start this procedure by setting the maquette and the wooden blank side by side, and standing back to have a good, long look at our progress. If we are happy with what we see, we

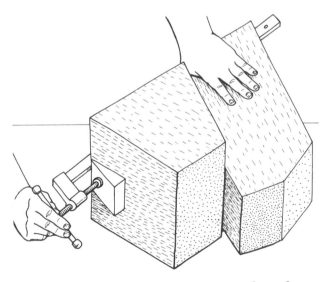

6–5 *If the component parts are uncomplicated, then it's easy enough to clamp up with a sash clamp and wedges. Nevertheless, always have a dry run to plan out the order of work—before using any glue.*

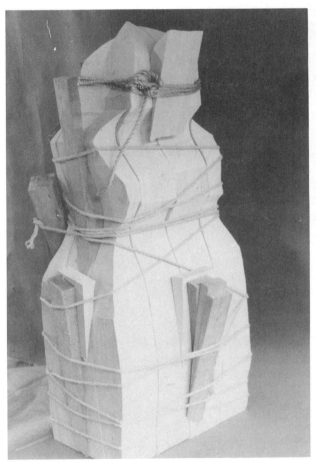

6–6 *If the shape to be glued and clamped is irregular, then it's best to use rope and wedges. All you do is lash the work up with rope—as tight as possible—and then bang in long, tapered wedges to pull the rope tight.*

6–7 *Front and side views of the roughed-out carving alongside the maquette.*

mark in on the faces of the wood all the obvious areas of waste that need to be cut back. So we might mark the sharp corners and any projections that we left on to help us with the clamping, and so on. We do this on all faces and views.

Having worked through this stage, we take one or another of our large, shallow-sweep, straight gouges and a mallet, and swiftly go over the whole workpiece cutting away the marked-in areas. We repeat this procedure several times—each time shading areas that need to be cut away, setting the workpiece and the maquette side by side, and then cutting back with the gouge (see **6–7**). And, of course, as we work through the repeats, so we use smaller and smaller gouges, with the cuts becoming smaller and more defined.

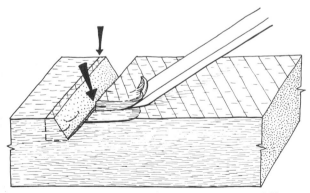

6–8 *A stop-cut acts as a barrier or stop to follow-up cuts. In this instance, it's plain to see that not only does the V-trench stop the split from running out of control, but, better yet, the strip of waste between the drawn line and the trench takes the brunt of any misplaced cuts.*

Setting-In Stop-Cuts

Having cleared away the bulk of the rough—meaning the waste—to the extent that the forms are more rounded, and most of the initial sawn faces have been cut back, then comes the stage of chopping in the primary stop-cuts. This is the point where you need to have a very clear image in your mind's eye as to how the finished carving is going to look. We say this because, up to this point, the procedures allow for a considerable degree of flexibility—the cuts and skims are so shallow that you can change the direction of the design. This is not so easy with the stop-cuts; once they have been made, then you have very little choice other than to waste the wood down to the level of that cut. The point we want to drive home is that as woodcarving is a process of removing layers—like peeling back the layers of an onion—once you have gone so far, then there is no going back. Okay, so you can glue a lump of wood on to replace a loss, but it's not easy. This being so, each successive stop-cut becomes more and more decisive.

The function of a stop-cut is literally to stop a cut (see **6–8**). For example, if you run a V-section stop-cut right across the face of the wood—so that there is precious wood to one side, and waste that needs to be lowered to the other—and then set about lowering the waste with a series of low skimming strokes—then the V-trench not only acts as a barrier to break the force of any strokes that overshoot, it also brings to a halt any splits or cuts that are set to run along the grain. As another example, with the under-sleeve fringe on the In-

6–9   Once the stop-cut has been made, you can use a mallet and chisel/gouge to swiftly clear the bulk of the waste. Note how, in this instance, we can even risk cutting in the direction of the grain.

6–10   When all the primary planes have been established—meaning all the main dips, humps, and hollows that go to make the design—then the roughing out is complete.

dian's buckskin, we first chopped a stop-cut down into the side of the arm—to mark the point where the fringe joins the arm—and then set the workpiece on its side and used a chisel to lower the face of the fringe. As you can see in **6–9**, it doesn't matter too much that the chisel is driven directly into end grain, because the stop-cut is going to brake the length of the cut.

Modelling

We find the modelling stage to be, at one and the same time, the most enjoyable, the most scary, and the most challenging. The rough has been cleared, the main lines of the design have been set-in with V-section grooves and stop-cuts, all the primary forms have been established, and we have to model the details (see **6–10**). Nearly finished, and yet so far to go! It's just as if all the "veils" have been lifted bar one. It's exciting because we can never quite be certain what we will find under the final veil, and it's scary because one badly judged move at this stage can mess up the whole carving.

While modelling is, in terms of technique, an uncomplicated wood-removing procedure, as already described in other sections, it is also a matter of taste, judgment, courage, and skill. Although the removal of wood is by this time a relatively easy business of making smaller and smaller skimming cuts with smaller and smaller tools, the degree to which such and such a detail is modelled does depend on what you personally bring to the carving. To our way of thinking, modelling is a process of continual assessment and self-questioning. Should the carving go in such and such a direction? Do we have the necessary skill to make the next stroke? Would it look better if we continued? Should we simply call a halt before we make a mess-up? Have we spent enough time on it already? We usually feel that if only we had the lacking courage/time/skill/energy to take it that little bit further, then it would be brilliant!

And so you continue with the modelling by looking; making another cut; skimming back more waste; defining such and such a detail (see **6–11**), until you figure the carving is finished.

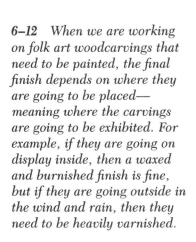

6–11 *A small sharp knife is a good tool for cleaning out creases and crisping up details.*

Finishing and Presentation

When you have taken the carving as far as you want it to go, or as far as you dare go, then pick up your finest and sharpest tools and a small brush, and set to work tidying up and finishing. This is the time when you need to ask a few questions: Do you want such and such a surface to be smooth? Or do you want to leave the marks made by the tools? Take a look at **6–12**; they are variously successful, but not because Gillian carved the Indian Chief and Alan carved the sailor—both carved in a naive, folksy style. In retrospect, we would both agree that the chief actually had looked so much better at the stage just before Gillian started sanding and smoothing, but we made the right choice on the sailor—being left with tool marks across the surfaces. The point is that you have a choice. Do you want to go for super-smooth unpainted surfaces with the pattern of grain enhancing them, do you want every tool mark to be on view, or do you maybe want to go for a mix of tooled, punched, and sanded textures?

Having skimmed and sanded to the extent that every surface and detail is at least in good shape—no splinters, dust, or ragged grain—then comes the time for the final finish.

6–12 *When we are working on folk art woodcarvings that need to be painted, the final finish depends on where they are going to be placed— meaning where the carvings are going to be exhibited. For example, if they are going on display inside, then a waxed and burnished finish is fine, but if they are going outside in the wind and rain, then they need to be heavily varnished.*

If you want the grain on view, all you do is brush with oil or wax, burnish to a finish, and the job is done. If you want it painted, then you need to seal the surface, lay on one or more undercoats of a color to suit, and then brush on the final colors. If you are interested in colored painted finishes, then look at our *Carving Figureheads and Other Nautical Designs*, also from STERLING PUBLISHING COMPANY.

Primary Tools and Proper Handling Techniques

All the tools and tool holding and handling techniques that are used in chip carving and relief carving—presented in those sections—are used to a greater or lesser extent in sculptural work, but the nature of sculptural carving calls for technique with a more flexible approach, the carver generally using a bigger range of tools and more complex vises and hold-downs.

Of course, we know full well that the tool, technique, and wood-holding problems that you will come up against will relate to your particular carving needs—your body size and strength, the location of your workshop, and the size, type, and scale of your carvings—but the following tips will get you set on the right course.

Tools for Sculpture

In our experience, most beginners have in mind to carve fairly sizable pieces of wood sculpture. In that case, you will need a good range of straight tools, a selection of bent and spoon tools that relate to your specific needs, and at least one mallet. For first roughing out we use a set of sculptor's firmer gouges that are designed to withstand repeated blows from the mallet (see **6–13**); we use a set of special high-quality German tools for general modelling (see **6–14**); and we use a handful of high-quality, large-size English tools for big work (see **6–15**).

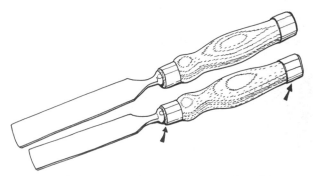

6–13   A firmer straight gouge is a good tool for heavy-duty roughing out—when you have to remove a lot of waste wood. If you are thinking of getting such a tool, it's best to go for one that has a leather washer between the shoulder of the tang and the handle—to absorb shock—and a hoop around the butt end of the handle—to prevent the wood handle from splitting.

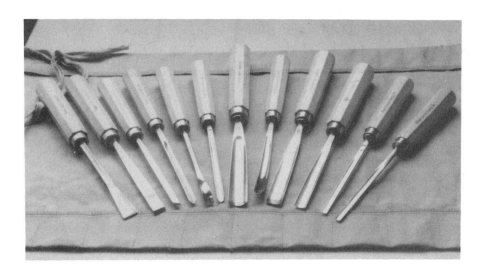

6–14   Many specialist suppliers are prepared to select individual tools, to make up sets to suit individual needs. This Lamp brand set is made up of twelve carefully honed, ready-to-use tools.

6–15 *Tools can be purchased either polished and honed and ready to use, or "in-the-black" and needing to be honed—as with the set shown. If you have doubts as to your needs, then seek the advice of a specialist supplier.*

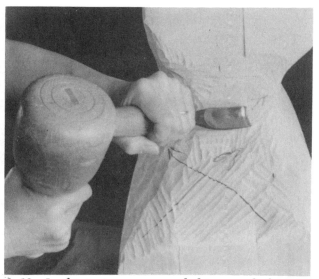

6–16 *In this instance, we needed to use a hefty gouge and mallet to remove the large areas of waste. Note the pencilled arrows that show the direction of cut.*

We are always wanting and lusting after more tools—we have seen the most desirable Japanese gouges, Swiss gouges, and Swedish gouges—all beautiful! The set of German gouges shown in **6–14** have been carefully selected as being a good range for beginners.

Roughing Out with Mallet and Gouge

To our way of thinking, there is nothing quite so pleasuresome as roughing out a good-size sculpture with a mallet and a sharp gouge. In many ways, it is a complete activity in itself—most therapeutic and restful—a bit like whittling a stick for no other reason than it is a good feeling to cut wood with a sharp blade. The blade does have to be sharp, you do have to be approaching the grain to best effect, and you do have to be working with a lively tap-tap-tapping of the mallet. Lots of small, ever-moving cuts and blows.

If you have a close-up look at **6–16** and **6–17**, you will see that, in both instances, we have had to modify our way of working to suit the run of the grain. For example, with the upright figure in **6–16**, we found that the best way of shaping up the waist and hips was to work from high to low grain in a spiral pattern around the form. We cut into the waist—first from the hips and around and

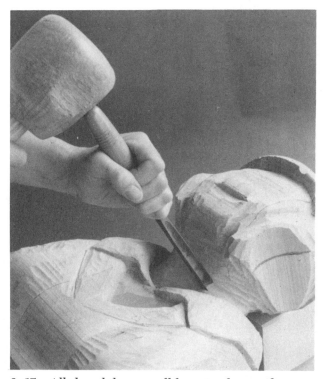

6–17 *All the while you will have to chop-and-change gouges to suit the work. In this instance, we found that the narrow valley of waste was best removed with a straight, deep U-section gouge. Up to a point, the more tools you have, then the easier it is to find a tool to suit the task at hand.*

down—and then from the bosom and around and down. We discovered that the act of running the spiral of cuts around the figure helped to ensure that the form was balanced, symmetrical, and nicely rounded. In both instances—with the waist of the female figure, and the neck of the sailor—it was necessary to select gouge sweeps and widths to fit the contours.

Thumb-Levering Skimming

This particular way of working with a gouge, as shown in **6–18**, means using both hands to increase the control and power of the cut. In use, the shallow-sweep straight gouge is held in one hand so that the butt of the handle is pushed hard into the palm, and then the other hand is set on the workpiece so that the thumb is pressing down on the blade. The working action involves keep-

ing the left hand fixed on the workpiece, and the thumb pressed down, while at the same time the tool is pushed forward and pivoted. We find that having both hands linked in this fashion not only controls the extent of the cuts, but also the seesawing, levering action that occurs under the thumb greatly increases the efficiency of the cut.

Thrusting and Levering

There are instances, as in **6–19**, when the power of the cut can be greatly increased by using some part of the workpiece as a levering fulcrum. Of course, much will depend on the context of the cut

6–18 *In this instance, I applied pressure with the thumb and took low shearing cuts to achieve the rolling shape of the collar.*

6–19 *The grasping, leveraged action not only ensures that the cutting edge is placed well on target, but it also maximizes the cutting efficiency by allowing the shaft of the tool to be levered against the workpiece.*

6–20 *Bent tools are used for skimming the waste from sunken areas. In this instance we used a wide tool for the bulk of the work, and a narrow tool for the tight angle at the top of the scroll.*

and the fragility of the wood around the area of the cut, but the act of levering is one way of making a small tight cut, while at the same time maximizing the efficiency. In use, the tool is pushed down with one hand, held hard up against the workpiece with the other, while at the same time the handle is pulled back so that the cutting edges run down in a tight scooping action. Working in this way, the leveraged action of the tool being held hard up against the wood, with the control of the encircling fingers right down near the blade, makes for a most efficient cut—much better than using a small gouge to run around the hollow.

Using a Spoon-Bent Tool

Spoon-bit and spoon-bent tools are designed specifically as skimming and scooping tools—just perfect for clearing the waste from tight angles, dips, and corners. In use, they are best held with one hand pushing and the other guiding, the fingers of the guiding hand also supplying additional pressure to the moving blade. Working in this way (see **6–20**), a good, sharp spoon-bent tool is easily capable of getting into tight spots and skimming the lowered ground to a smooth finish.

We nearly always use a gouge as a preferred option to the chisel, for the double reason that while the corners of the spoon-bent chisel tend to scratch the surface and generally get in the way, the gouge leaves an attractive dappled surface.

If you are a beginner, and are looking to purchase a single bent tool, then a good all-rounder is a No. 17 sweep at about ⅜in (10mm) wide.

Making a Precise Modelling Cut

The modelling stage requires that the cuts are well placed. Or to put it another way, while you can afford to make mess-ups at the roughing-out stage, the nearer you get to finishing, then the smaller the room for error. And, of course, there is an argument for saying that every cut needs to be perfectly targeted. All that aside, once you have mastered the various tricks and techniques that have to do with holding the wood, keeping the tools sharp, and approaching the grain to best effect, then all that is left is being able to use the tools to best effect. In that context, the nipping, modelling cut is a very useful hold. In action, the tool is held in one hand, with the butt of the handle hard into the palm and the index finger

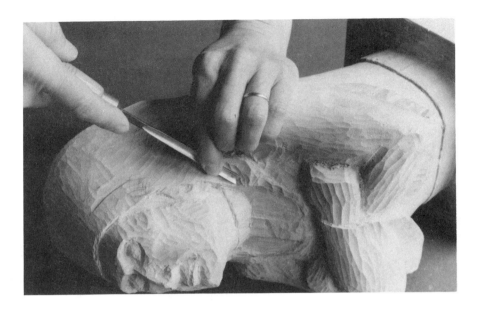

6–21 *Using the pinched fingers as a fulcrum—like the midpoint under a seesaw—the gouge can be worked with a super-efficient shearing cut. In use, the pinched fingers hold the tool while the handle is "paddled" from side to side.*

running down the shaft; the thumb and index finger of the other hand are used to guide and restrain the cut. By pivoting the tool between the pinching finger and thumb so that the cutting edge slides at an angle across the wood, the levering efficiency is much increased (see **6–21**).

Making a Paring Shaving Cut

Although making a paring shaving cut with a gouge might look to be inefficient, awkward, and perhaps even dangerous (see **6–22**, left), it is, in fact, a very useful way of working. In use, the tool is held in much the same way as you would hold a crooked knife—in other words, the gouge is

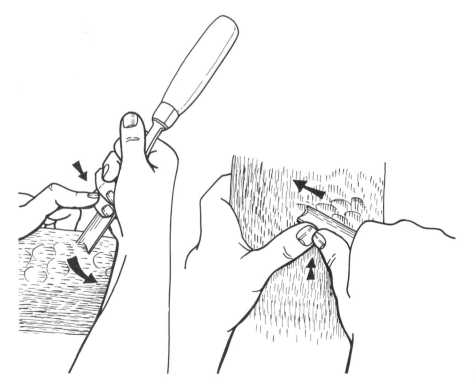

6–22 *(Left) To make a paring cut, grasp the gouge in a dagger-like grip, brace the tool with the other hand, and then make a tightly controlled slicing or shearing cut towards your body. (Right) A modified paring cut can be used to remove fine slivers of wood. More or less the same procedures are taking place— the only real difference is that the cut is being made away from the body.*

6-23 *Making an undercut. (Left) First define the depth of the cut by slicing down-and-around the area being modelled. (Right) Clean out the waste by running a bent tool along the lowered ground and into the initial defining cut.*

Repeat both procedures until the undercut is at the required depth.

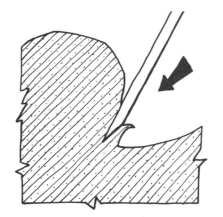
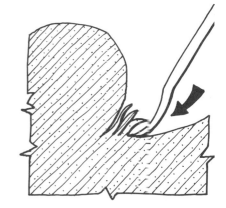

gripped like a dagger, with the blade being more or less pointed at your body, and then the blade is "paddled" and pared with a swivelling, stirring wrist action. This way of working is good on, at least, two counts—it is a very efficient way of skimming a surface to a good finish, and it is safe.

Making Chisel and Gouge Undercuts

Although making deep undercuts is thought of by many beginners as being somewhat tricky, it is, in fact, a straightforward procedure—or, we should add, as long as you are mindful that undercutting is generally a business of making two strokes. First, a primary stop-cut is made to define the depth of the undercut, and then this is followed up with a second stroke to meet the stop-cut (see **6–23**). It's much easier to do than to describe. Of course, depending on the size, shape, and location of the area to be worked, you might well have to keep chopping and changing the tools to suit.

Using a V-section Tool on End Grain

Although we generally prefer to make V-section trenches with two or three cuts of the knife, this is not so easy when working on end grain. In such a situation, where the knife is likely to run into the grain, or the wood is so hard and dense that we can't make a mark, we find that using a V-tool is sometimes the only way to make progress. In use, the depth of the trench is achieved by making a series of cuts—one cut to mark out the route, and subsequent cuts to make the trench deeper and wider (see **6–24**). The good news is that V-tools "enjoy" cutting across hard, dense wood!

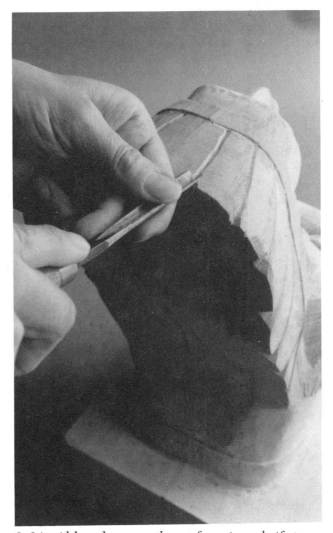

6-24 *Although we mostly opt for using a knife to make V-cuts, a V-tool is best used when cutting across end grain. In the context of carving this chiefs war bonnet, we also needed to use a mallet.*

Slicing with a Knife

In instances where you want to cut and define a deep crease that runs into end grain, as on the scroll in **6–25**, then the best procedure is to make a series of knife cuts one on top of the other. While working in this way results in the waste coming away as slivers, it also minimizes the risk of splitting the wood. It's not so easy on hard wood, but it's great on soft, easy-to-carve wood like linden/lime and basswood.

6–25 *We find that, in a good many situations, a knife is the best tool for getting into difficult-to-reach creases. In this context we made repeated slicing cuts to define and refine a deep undercut.*

Beginner's Workout

Though sculptural carving is a subject so vast that there are innumerable and limitless possibilities as to style, form, tradition, size, and function, we feel that, in terms of technique at least, it can be boiled down to the three basic stages: blocking out the image as seen in two views; rounding and roughing out; and modelling. Of course, having an understanding of the aims and goals of these primary technique stages, and being fully cognizant of the tool and material implications of working through the various options and knowing how to use such and such a tool, won't make you a woodcarver, but taken all together, these skills and understandings will go a long way towards enabling you to make confident choices as to the best way to proceed.

The following linked sequence of exercises will help you on your way.

Blocking Out with a Flexible-Bladed Saw

You need a bench with a vise and the use of a small band saw—or you could use a large scroll saw, a bow saw, or a coping saw.

Take a 12in (30.5cm) length of square section, easy-to-carve wood at about 3in (7.6cm) square, and draw out the three forms on the faces of the wood as shown in **6–26**—the circle, the square, and the rectangle. Then work through the exercise, as presented in the caption to **6–26**, by shading in the waste you want to remove, clearing away the main areas using a handsaw, and finally clearing away the secondary waste.

Roughing Out and Rounding

You need a couple of narrow-width straight gouges, a bent gouge, a drill, and sandpaper.

Having worked through the previous exercise, stay with the same piece of wood, and use the gouges to rough out the basic shape. Perhaps the form isn't too exciting, but if you can successfully rough out the shape of the ball, cube, and cylinder, then you are well on the way to knowing what you are doing (see **6–27**).

6-26 *Blocking-out exercise. (Left) Take your chosen square-section length of easy-to-carve wood, and set it out on all four faces—with a circle, a square, and a rectangle. Note that the size of the square and the circle will, of course, be governed by the section of your chosen piece of wood. Shade in the waste so that you know clearly what you intend to remove. (Middle) Use a small handsaw to clear the primary areas of waste from one side face. If you can speed this stage up by using, say, a band saw, then so much the better. (Right) As to how you clear the small pieces of secondary waste from the other face, this will in part depend on the size of your carving. If it's small you could use a knife or you could maybe follow though and use the saw. By the time you have finished this stage, all four side profiles should look more or less identical.*

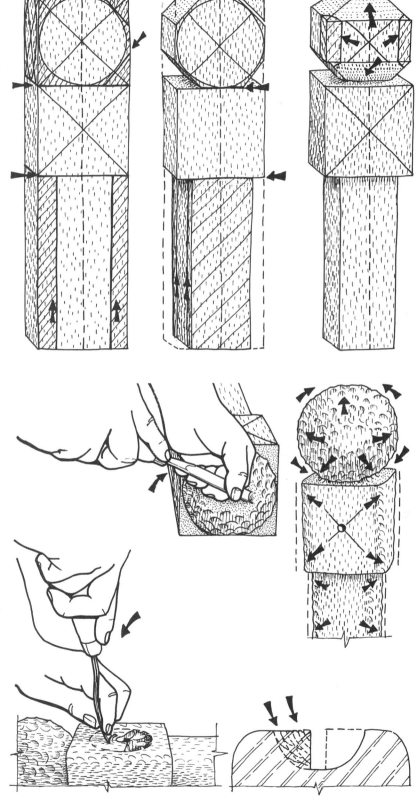

6-27 *Roughing and rounding exercise. (Top, left, and right) Having secured the workpiece in the vise, or maybe with a clamp, take a small, straight gouge and set to work skimming off the sawn faces. All the while you are working, be sure to cut either with or at an angle to the grain— never try to cut directly into end grain. If you are doing it right, you will always be cutting from high to low wood. (Bottom, left, and right) When you come to carve the depression—the little hollow—on one or all sides of the cube, first set the depth of the depression by drilling a guide hole, and then follow through with a bent tool. Start carving hard up against the drilled hole, and then back up, all the while cutting the hole deeper and deeper. Be mindful that you must never cut into end grain.*

Modelling

You need a shallow-sweep straight gouge, a bent gouge, a knife, and sandpaper.

When we were in art school, the sculptor told us to carve a cube linked to a sphere; we all probably had the same thought—how easy, how boring, and how silly! But it wasn't and it isn't.

And just in case you are thinking that this form looks a bit like a figure or a doll, then you are correct—it is just that. As we see it, if you can carve this stylized archetypal figure, then you are well on the way to being able to carve a doll, a large figure, or a mother and child—the possibilities are endless (see **6–28**).

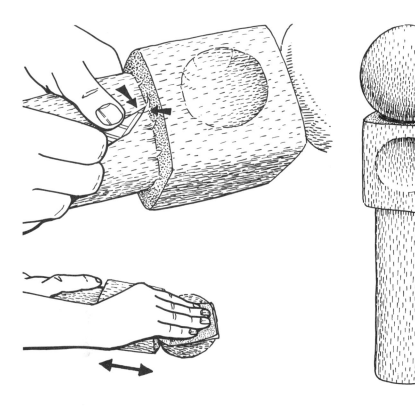

6–28 *Modelling exercise. Once you are happy with the roughing-out stage, take a small knife and generally work around the carving, cleaning up. We usually start with a large knife and finish up with a scalpel. If you feel the need to have the carving super-smooth, then work through the grades of sandpaper— from rough to fine.*

Chapter 7

PROJECTS

A Rustic Country Stool

Techniques   Adze, knife, and gouge work.

Tools
- use of a band saw
- couple of straight gouges
- drawknife
- small adze
- crooked knife

- hooked knife
- drill with a 1⅛in (28mm) diameter Forstner bit
- all the usual workshop items like a pencil, ruler, sandpaper, glue, mallet, bench, and vise

Cutting List
- 1½in (3.8cm) thick slab of oak 21in (53.3cm) long and 15in (38cm) wide for the seat—best if it has plenty of character (see **7–1**)
- 1½in (3.8cm) thick slab of oak 21in (53.3cm) long and 6in (15.2cm) wide for the legs

7–1   *Project picture.*

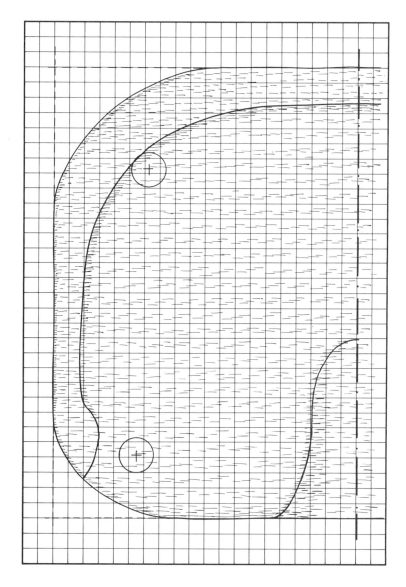

7–2 *Working drawing—at a grid scale of two squares to one inch.*

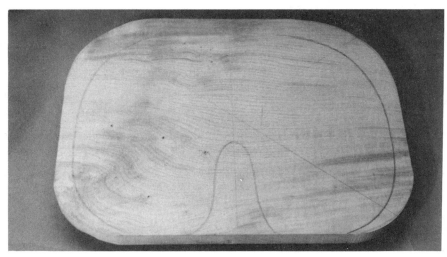

7–3 *The seat slab marked out with the lines of the design and cut to shape.*

7–4 *The blanks—four legs and the seat slab.*

Making the Seat

1. Take the slab of prepared 1½in (3.8cm) thick oak, check it over just to make sure that it's in good condition, and pencil-mark the various sides and faces so that you know what you are planning to do.

2. Trace the design (see **7–2**), and transfer the traced lines to the top face of the seat slab. Don't worry at this stage about the position of the leg holes.

3. Run the wood through the band saw and cut away the corners of waste. Aim for an overall symmetrical profile, aligned on a centerline that runs from front to back of the seat. While the saw is at hand, slice the four legs to size (see **7–3** and **7–4**).

4. Flip the seat slab over so that the back or bottom is uppermost, and use either a gouge or drawknife to swiftly run a chamfer around the underside of the edge (see **7–5**). Aim for a chamfer of about ¼in (6mm). Make sure that you only cut in the direction of the grain—meaning from the front/back of the seat slab and around towards the end.

7-5 *Cut a chamfer around the underside of the seat slab.*

5. Set the slab in the vise, and use the drawknife to round-over the top edge. Aim for a small chamfer along the front edge, and a generous round-over along the back and sides (see **7–6**).

6. Having used the drawknife and the gouge to round-over the slab at the back and sides, then use the small adze to hollow carve the two cheeks, or saddle hollows, and the central codpiece. See how we needed to work this way and that to approach the wild grain to best advantage (see **7–7**).

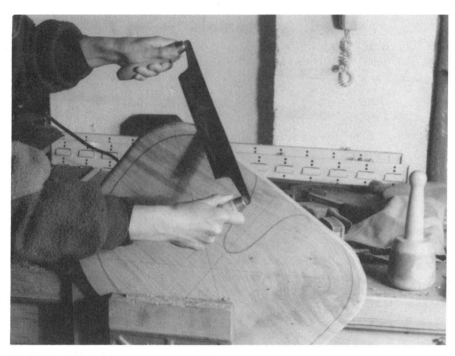

7–6 *Use the drawknife to shape the top edge of the seat slab.*

7–7 *Use the adze to rough out the shape of the seat saddle and codpiece. Notice how we needed to work this way and that to approach the wild grain to best advantage.*

7. Once you have removed the bulk of the waste with the gouge, variously use the crooked knife (see **7–8**) and the hooked knife (see **7–9**) to carve and shave the seat hollows to shape.

Make it your intention to run the hollows off at the front edge of the seat, and to leave the whole area looking clean and smooth—the smoother the better.

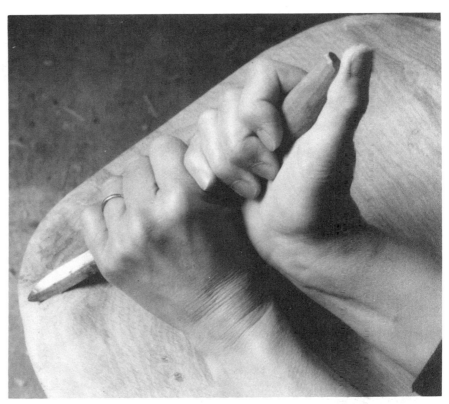

7–8   Use the crooked knife to skim the face of the seat to a good finish.

7–9   Use the hooked knife to carve and scrape difficult twisted-grain areas.

7–10 *Cut the legs to shape with the drawknife.*

7–11 *Make repeated tests for a good, tight push fit.*

Making and Fitting the Legs

8. Having swiftly cut the wood down so that you have four leg sticks at 1½in (3.8cm) square, set them one at a time in the vise, and chamfer them from bottom to top with the drawknife (see **7–10**).

9. Skim off all four corners of the square leg so that the upper end of the leg is octagonal in section—and so that the chamfer starts at a point at floor level, and gradually widens as it travels up the length of the leg. Shave the top end of the leg so that it's a tight push fit in a 1⅛in (2.8cm) diameter hole. Drill a hole through a piece of scrap wood and test for a good fit (see **7–11**).

10. Mark out the position of the four leg holes on the top face of the seat slab—as shown in the working drawing, **7–2**—and then use the drill and 1⅛in (2.8cm) diameter Forstner bit to bore out the four holes. Although you can make a jig to ensure that the splay of the four legs is correct, we find that the best method is to drill the first hole by eye, set one of the legs

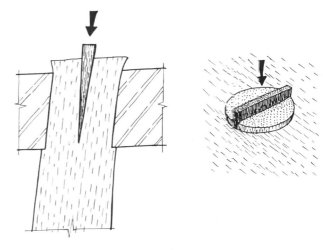

7–13   Glue and wedge the legs.

in the first hole as shown in **7–12**, and then use it as a guide to angle the other holes. As you can see, the isosceles triangle between the drill, the seat, and the leg ensures that the splay of the legs is well matched.

11. Having cut all four legs to shape, and had a dry run fitting, make a narrow V-cut about 1in (2.5cm) down into the top of the legs, and glue and wedge as shown in **7–13**. Make sure that the legs are set so that the wedge runs at right angles to the seat grain.

12. Finally, once the glue is dry, shave the leg tops and wedges off flush with the top of the seat, use the fine-grade sandpaper to rub down to a smooth finish, and burnish with clear beeswax furniture polish.

Afterthoughts

- If you haven't got a band saw, you could use a bow saw or a coping saw to cut the seat slab.
- It's a good idea to mark the top end of the leg with the 1⅛in (2.8cm) bit—we drilled a hole about 1/16in (1.5mm) deep—and then you will have a guide diameter to work to when you are shaving the leg to shape and size with the drawknife.
- Traditionally, chairmakers either used a reamer to cut the seat holes to a tapered section and/or they cut a stepped spigot—a round tenon—on the top end of the leg.

7–12   Drill the four through-holes from the top of the seat slab.

Ball-in-a-Cage Puzzle

Techniques   Knife work, for whittling and chip carving

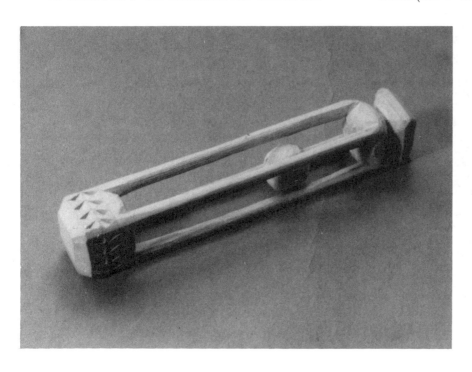

Tools
- selection of small sharp-point knives
- pair of compasses
- all the usual workshop items like a pencil, ruler, and sandpaper

Cutting List
- 6in (15.2cm) length of 1in (2.5cm) square section of easy-to-carve wood—we used linden/lime

Setting-Out the Design

1. Before you do anything else, check your wood over and make sure that it is completely straight-grained and free from knots and splits.

2. Study the project picture (see **7–14**) and the working drawings (see **7–15**), and note how the whole design is based on a grid at a scale of four grid squares to one inch.

3. Take a pencil and ruler, and set the wood out as shown in **7–16**. Establish the end center-points by drawing crossed diagonals, set lines ¼in (6mm) in from the edges of the side faces, fix the centerpoint halfway along the 6in (15.2cm) length, set out the three 1in (2.5cm) blocks—one at each end and one at the center—mark out the position of the decorative grooves and the chip carving, and shade in the areas that need to be cut away.

Cutting the Ball

4. Having studied the various drawings and photographs, take a small knife and sink the drawn lines in with stop-cuts—that is, repeatedly score the lines until the main cage is established (see **7–16**, bottom left).

5. Rework the stop-cuts on all four sides of the wood until they are sunk to a depth of a little over ⅛in (3mm) (see **7–16**, top left). It's all easy enough as long as you are mindful that as the bars of the cage will finish up about ½ to ⅝in (1.3 to 1.6cm) apart, so must the ball not be smaller than, say, ¾in (1.9cm) in diameter.

6. With the stop-cut lines in place along the length of the wood, repeat the procedure at the ends of the cage. Do this on all sides of the wood (see **7–16**, right).

7–14   Project picture.

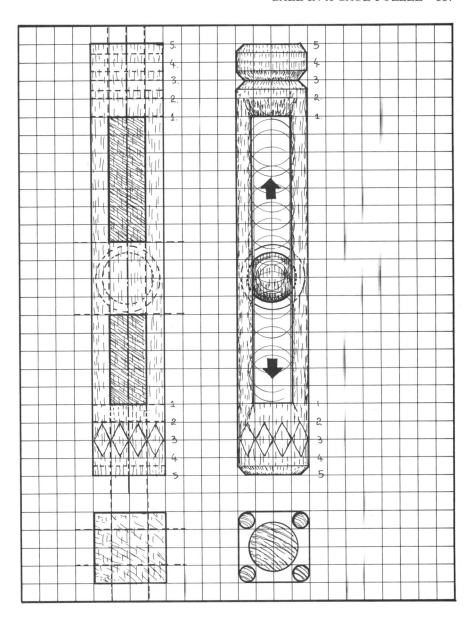

7–15 *Working drawing—at a scale of four grid squares to one inch.*

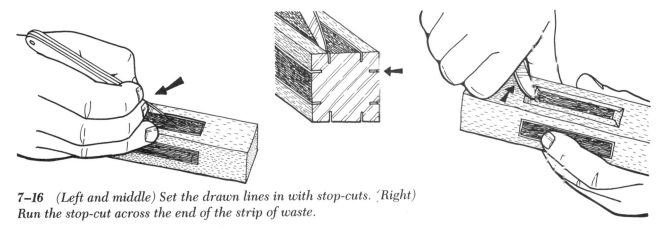

7–16 *(Left and middle) Set the drawn lines in with stop-cuts. (Right) Run the stop-cut across the end of the strip of waste.*

7. When you reach a point where the ball section is more or less free of the bars, carefully slide the point of the knife in at an angle to nip around underneath the bar. Clear a little sliver of waste so that you can just about see light between the bar and the lump of wood in the middle (see **7–17**, top right).

8. Having sliced through along the underside of the bar, remove repeated chips of waste at top and bottom of the ball—until the whole ball lump is able to slide up and down within the cage (see **7–17**, top left). You have reached the stage where your aim shifts from simply removing waste to shaping the ball.

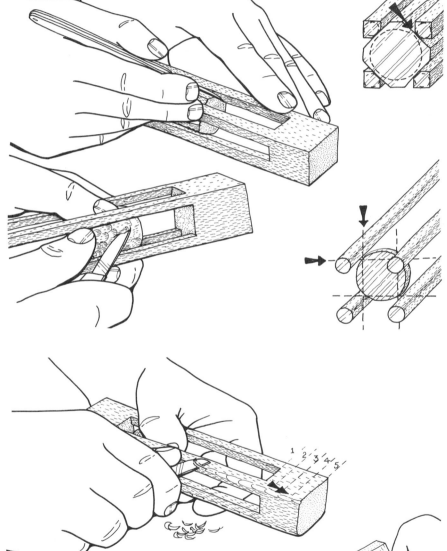

7–17   *(Top right) Slice under the bar. (Top left) Clear the waste from either end of the cage. (Bottom left) Shape the ball. (Bottom right) Carve the ball and the bars to a round section.*

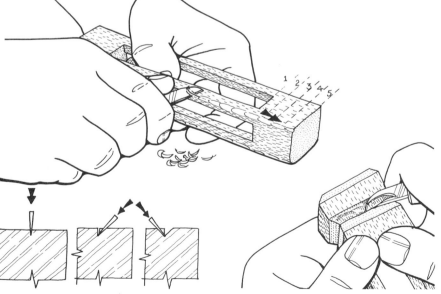

7–18   *(Top) Clean up the bars and number the guide lines. (Bottom left, left to right) The three cuts that go to make a V-section trench. (Bottom right) Cut the V-trench and the end chamfer.*

9. Gently remove the waste at either end of the lump, and pare away until the ball takes shape (see **7–17**, bottom left). Continue until the ball is able to turn and roll freely within the cage. Finally, skim and shave both the ball and the bars until they are more or less round in cross section (see **7–17**, bottom right and **7–18**, top).

Cutting the Incised Lines

10. When you have carved the ball and cage to shape and brought it to a good, smooth finish, take another look at the working drawing (see **7–15**) and see how the decorative features— the grooves at one end and the chip carving at the other—are based on a primary ¼in (6mm) grid. Set each end of the wood out with the grid, and number the lines 1, 2, 3, 4 and 5— as shown in **7–18**, top.

11. Starting at the incised end, take your knife and sink line No. 3 with a ⅛in (3mm) deep stop-cut. This done, make secondary cuts at an angle into the stop-cut to achieve a V-section trench (see **7–18**, bottom left).

12. Deepen and widen the V-trench until each side of the "V" is ⅛in (3mm) wide, and run a ⅛in bevel around the end of the wood (see **7–18**, bottom right).

Chip Carving

13. Having already set the chip-carved end out with the grid and numbered the lines (see **7–19**), as already described, divide up the two middle bands of squares to have eight isosceles triangles centered and mirror-imaged on line No. 3 (see **7–15** and **7–20**, bottom). Do this on all four faces of the wood.

14. To make a chip cut, the sequence is to stab the "V" in with two straight-down stabbing cuts, and then to clear the triangle of waste with a low, skimming cut (see **7–20**, top, left to right).

15. Finally, having cleared all 32 triangles— eight on each face of the wood—rub the wood swiftly over with the sandpaper, and the project is finished.

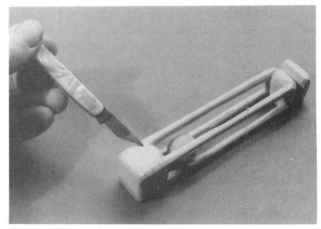

7–19 *Set out the grid lines that go to make up the design.*

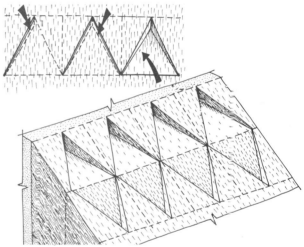

7–20 *(Top, left to right) The three cuts that go to make a triangular chip. (Bottom) The layout and shape of the eight chip cuts.*

Afterthoughts

• Since the whole project hinges on the wood being easy to carve, you need to choose your wood with care. We have gone for linden/lime, but you could just as well go for a wood like basswood, holly, or sycamore.

• Your knife must be razor sharp.

• If you have any doubts as to the procedures, you could have a trial run with a block of hard soap or Plasticine.

• If you are brave, you could have more than one ball in the cage!

A Wildfowl Decoy

Techniques Gouge, chisel, and knife, carving in the round, a long-billed curlew

Tools

- use of a band saw—big enough to cut through 4in (10.2cm) thick wood
- use of a workbench with a holdfast
- ¾in (19mm) wide shallow-sweep straight gouge
- mallet
- knife
- drill and a selection of Forstner bits
- rasp
- selection of acrylic paints in muted colors such as dark brown, dark leaf green, blue-grey, and brown-orange
- wax polish
- all the usual workshop items like a pencil, ruler, and sandpaper

Cutting List

- 18in (45.7cm) length of easy-to-carve 4in (10.2cm) square section wood—we used linen/lime, but you could just as well use basswood
- couple of scraps of plum at about ¾in (19mm) thick—12in (30.5cm) long for the bill and 6in (15.2cm) long for the leg
- slab of found wood for the base—we used a bit found on a beach—it might be teak

Setting-Out the Design and Cutting the Blank

1. When you have carefully studied our project picture (see **7–21**) and working drawing (see **7–22**), draw the two views of the body at full size, and make clear tracings. You need both views shown in the working drawing. While you are at it, draw out the profile of the bill.

2. Having checked that the wood is free from such flaws as splits, knots, and the like, pencil-press transfer the traced "side" and "top" views to the 4in (10.2cm) square wood. Make sure that the tail and bill ends of the two views are aligned one with another. Shade in the waste wood that needs to be cut away.

3. Pass the wood through the band saw and cut the image out as seen in one view, then reassemble the block and repeat the procedure to cut it out as seen in the other view (see **7–23**). If you have done it right, you should finish up with the blank at the middle of the wood, and ten or so pieces of waste (see **7–24**).

7–21 *Project picture.*

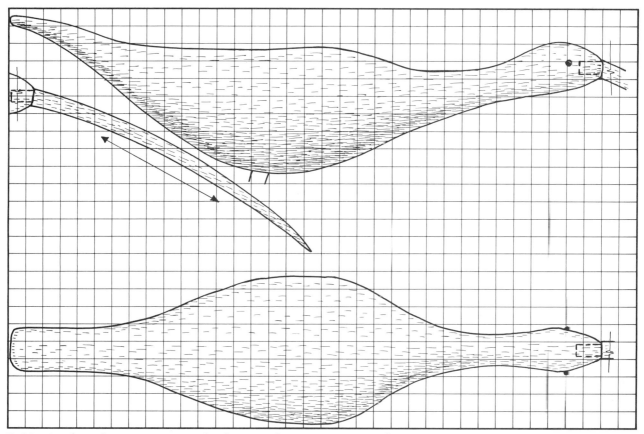

7–22 *Working drawing—at a scale of two grid squares to one inch.*

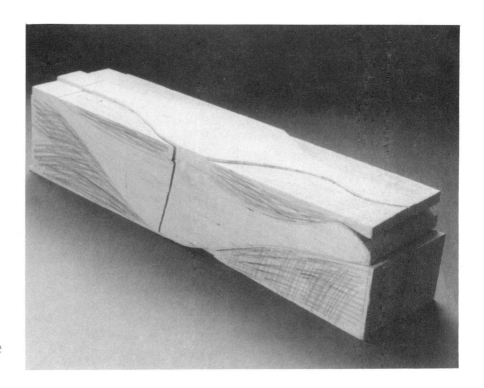

7–23 *Use the band saw to cut the form out in two views—first one view and then the other. Take a look at the results in* **7–24** *on the next page.*

7–24 *If you have done it right, there will be a minimum of short grain.*

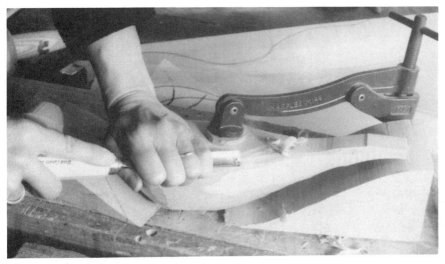

7–25 *With the workpiece cradled on the wedges of scrap and held in place with the holdfast, use the straight gouge to swiftly remove the rough.*

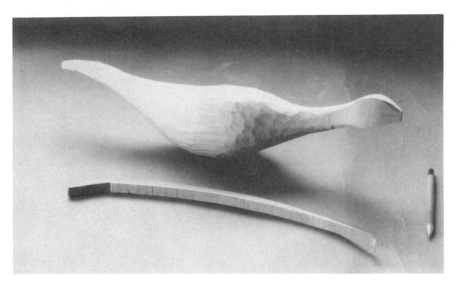

7–26 *Having first made sure that the design is placed so that there is a minimum of short grain, fret out the bill on the band saw.*

Roughing Out and Fitting the Bill

4. With the blank well supported and held secure on the bench—we used the waste bits of wood and a holdfast (see **7–25**)—take the straight gouge, and set to work clearing the areas of secondary waste. Work from the center through to the end—to avoid cutting into end grain; that is, from the bulge of the body to the tail, and to the head.

5. When you have cleared most of the rough—to the extent that the whole body form is more or less rounded in cross section—pencil-press transfer the drawn and traced shape of the bill to the wood. Make sure that the bill shape is placed and cut so that there is a minimum of short grain (see **7–22**). When you are happy with the placing, swiftly cut it out on the band saw (see **7–26**).

6. Use a knife to whittle the bill to a rough shape, and to cut a stepped spigot—or round tenon—on the head end. Aim for a tenon length of about ¾in (1.9cm), with a diameter to fit a drill size of between ¼ and ⅜in (6 and 10mm) (see **7–27**). Be mindful that the success of the project hinges on the angle of the bill to the head being just so. The two parts need to look as if they have grown together—like a plant shoot springing out of the ground.

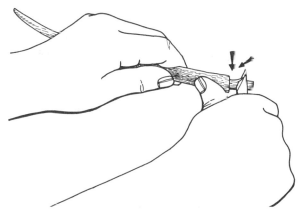

7–27   *Use a knife to whittle the bill to size and shape. Whittle a spigot—round tenon—to match your drill size, set the length of the tenon with a stop-cut, and then remove the waste with long, low skimming cuts.*

7. Having first double-checked that the angle of entry is correct, bore a hole about 1in (2.5cm) into the front of the head. When you have achieved a tight push fit of the bill tenon into the head mortise, smear a generous amount of glue on mating faces and set the bill in place (see **7–28**). While the tools and materials are at hand, run a hole up into the underside of the body and set the whole sculpture up on a single carved leg and a stand. Don't glue the leg into the body at this stage.

7–28   *Drill the hole into the head and trim the tenon for a tight push fit. As needed, modify the head-to-bill angle by adjusting the tenon.*

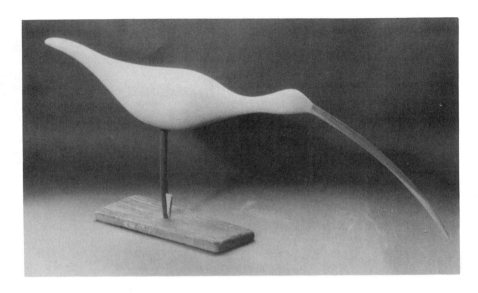

7–29 *Having rubbed the whole form to a smooth finish, glue the single leg into the stand, and get ready for painting.*

Finishing

8. Having waited until the glue is good and dry, use the knife, rasp, and sandpaper to rub the whole form down to a smooth-curved finish. Don't try for realism, just go for a stylized form, with the body, head, and bill all running smoothly one into another (see **7–29**). Work through the grades of sandpaper, from rough to fine, until all of the surfaces are smooth to the touch.

9. Once you are happy with the finish, wipe away the dust, and give the body of the bird an all-over wash of gold-brown acrylic paint. Follow this up with a muted green-brown wash on the top of the head at each side.

10. Take the fine-grade sandpaper and rub through the wash at wear points—at either side of the belly and throat, and on top of the tail.

11. Mix two more colors—a deep muted brown and a deep muted green—and dot and dash the whole body from the tail to the head, the dots and dashes getting smaller as you get towards the head.

12. Finally, rub through the paint at wear areas, push a couple of black ball-head dress-making pins in for the eyes, burnish with wax, glue fix the body to the support leg, and the job is done!

Afterthoughts

- As the success of this project has to do with the subtle relationship and coming together of the head and the bill, it's a good idea to make a Plasticine maquette.
- The choice of wood for the bill and the single leg is most important—it needs to be strong and close-grained. We chose English plum, but you could just as well go for cherry or yew.
- We tried using a shop-bought white wood dowel for the leg—it looked awful!
- Ideally, the base needs to be simple and understated.

Glossary of Woodcarving Terms

(Consult the Index for specific tools.)

Blank A block, slab, or disc of prepared wood—a piece of wood that has been prepared for carving.

Blocking in To draw the lines of a design onto the face of the wood and to establish the primary details of the pattern or form.

Burnishing The act of taking a piece of woodcarving to a hard, high-shine finish.

Chip carving A technique for decorating the surface of a carving by chipping out little triangular pockets.

Close-grained Wood that has narrow annual growth rings—such woods usually carve well.

Designing Working out a structure, pattern, or form by making sketches, outlines, and models and/or making prototypes that relate to museum originals.

Elevations In drawing, the views of an object. So a particular view might be described as "top," "end," or "side" elevation.

End grain Cross-section grain at the end of a piece of timber. End grain is difficult to carve, and so needs to be approached with care.

Finishing The act of scraping, rubbing down with sandpaper, painting, waxing, burnishing, and otherwise enhancing the appearance of a project.

First cuts Meaning the very first stages in the carving after the initial designing, drawing, and transferring has been done.

Found wood Taken to mean wood that can be found, beachcombed, or salvaged.

Grain Meaning the annual rings that run though the wood—all the lines, colors, and textures that characterize a piece of wood. Woodcarvers spend most of their time trying to angle the thrust and direction of their tools so as to cut the grain to best advantage. Ideally the woodcarver cuts either across or at a slight angle to the run of the grain.

Green wood Wood that still contains sap—unseasoned wood that is worked before it has dried out.

Gridded working drawing A scaled, square grid placed over a working drawing—in use, the object illustrated can be reduced or enlarged simply by changing the scale of the grid. For example, if the grid is described as "one square to one inch," and you want to double the scale, then all you do is read off each square as being equal to two inches. When you come to transferring the drawing to the wood, you just draw out a grid at the suggested size and directly transfer the contents of each square. At one square to one inch you draw out a full-size inch grid—at one square to two inches you draw out a full-size two-inch grid, and so on.

Grounding or wasting The act of cutting away the wood in and around the main design and taking it down to a lower level so that the design is left in relief.

Hardwood Botanically speaking, hardwood comes from broadleafed deciduous trees. Hardwood isn't necessarily harder to work than a softwood, but rather it is a term that describes general characteristics.

Hollow-carved or dished Meaning areas that have been lowered and modelled so that the resultant cavity is curved and dish-like in form.

Incised A shallow, knife-worked V-section trench or scoop cut. You first make an initial stop-cut, and then cut at an angle into each side of the stop-cut so as to remove a tapered V-section sliver of waste.

Kerf-cut In the context of this book, a partial cut made by a saw and/or a chisel and knife.

Knot These are termed as dead, hollow, loose, spiked, encased, and so on. Knots are unpredictable, so do your best to avoid them.

Lowering Meaning to cut away background wood to leave the design in high relief. This can also be termed grounding or wasting.

Maquette A working model—it could be made of clay, Plasticine, or scrap wood.

Marking out Using a sharp-pointed pencil to make crisp, clear, smooth-curved guide lines.

Modelling The act of carving a design to completion—the carving process of shaping the wood.

Off-cuts Small pieces of usable wood that are left over after you have made the project.

Pencil-press transferring The act of tracing a master design and then pressing the tracing onto the workpiece so that the lines of the design are transferred to the wood.

Piercing To drill, fret, or cut wood away so that only a tracery remains.

Plateau wood When the ground wood in and around a design feature has been cut away and lowered, the resultant remaining high-relief flat-topped feature might be termed a plateau. Many woodcarvers use geographical or topographical terms to describe various features—valleys, peaks, cliffs, beds.

Profile A form, blank, or cutout might be called a profile—this is also used to describe the flat, silhouette, or side view just after the waste has been cleared and just prior to modelling.

Roughing out The act of swiftly clearing away the bulk of the waste with a saw or large gouge—the carving stage prior to modelling.

Rubbing down or sanding The act of using an abrasive sandpaper/tool to rub the wood down to a good finish.

Scale The ratio between the working drawing and the carving to be made. In use, you read off the scale—for example, "one grid square to one inch"—then you draw up a full-size one-inch grid and transfer the contents of the working drawing squares to your full-size squares.

Seasoned wood   Wood that is considered to have a low and workable moisture content. One woodcarver's seasoned wood could well be another woodcarver's useless over-dry scrap.

Setting-in   Meaning to cut in along the design line and to separate the ground wood from the relief design.

Setting-out   The act of transferring the traced lines to the wood and generally preparing the wood, the tools, and the working area prior to carving.

Shallow relief carved   Areas that have been wasted and lowered to a shallow depth. A design that travels over the surface of a carving without changing the primary shape of the piece.

Short-grain   Meaning areas of wood where the structure of the grain is such that the wood is fragile and liable to split.

Stop-cut   An initial cut straight down into the wood—a cut into which secondary cuts are made. A stop-cut defines the length of subsequent cuts and acts as a brake; it literally stops the cut.

Tooled finish   Meaning a finish that is textured with the marks left by the tools.

Trenching   The procedure of sinking a stop-cut and then using a knife or V-section tool to cut into each side of the stop-cut so as to remove a sliver of waste.

Undercutting   The act of sinking the waste to make a plateau, and then to gouge out a cavity from the side of the plateau to achieve an overhang or undercut.

Waste ground   The areas in and around the design that need to be lowered, wasted, and otherwise cut away.

Whittling   Generally taken to mean cutting and carving with a small hand-held knife.

Working drawing   A scaled and detailed drawing—one that shows sizes, sections, details, etc. Never cut the original drawings; always take a tracing, and keep the drawing as a master.

Working face   The best side of the wood—the side on which you have drawn the shapes—the front of the panel; the outside panels of the box—the face that is in full view.

Metric Conversion

Feet and Inch Conversions

| 1 inch = 25.4mm |
| 1 foot = 304.8mm |

Metric Conversions

| 1 mm = 0.039 inch |
| 1 m = 3.28 feet |

| mm = millimetre |
| m = metre |

Inches to Millimetres and Centimetres						
mm—millimetres			cm—centimetres			
inches	mm	cm	inches	cm	inches	cm
⅛	3	0.3	9	22.9	30	76.2
¼	6	0.6	10	25.4	31	78.7
⅜	10	1.0	11	27.9	32	81.3
½	13	1.3	12	30.5	33	83.8
⅝	16	1.6	13	33.0	34	86.4
¾	19	1.9	14	35.6	35	88.9
⅞	22	2.2	15	38.1	36	91.4
1	25	2.5	16	40.6	37	94.0
1¼	32	3.2	17	43.2	38	96.6
1½	38	3.8	18	45.7	39	99.1
1¾	44	4.4	19	48.3	40	101.6
2	51	5.1	20	50.8	41	104.1
2½	64	6.4	21	53.3	42	106.7
3	76	7.6	22	55.9	43	109.2
3½	89	8.9	23	58.4	44	111.8
4	102	10.2	24	61.0	45	114.3
4½	114	11.4	25	63.5	46	116.8
5	127	12.7	26	66.0	47	119.4
6	152	15.2	27	68.6	48	121.9
7	178	17.8	28	71.1	49	124.5
8	203	20.3	29	73.7	50	127.0

Index

About the Authors

ALAN AND GILL (for Gillian) Bridgewater, a unique husband-and-wife team, have gained an international reputation as producers of crafts books of the highest calibre. Concentrating on woodwork, woodcarving, and folk art, they are regarded internationally as authorities on Pacific Northwest Native American totems and masks, toys, chip carving, misericords, carved and painted furniture, and nautical carving. The perfect partnership: Gill does all the step-by-step illustrations, Alan does the technical illustrations and writes the text, and they both roll up their sleeves for the hands-on crafts.

The Bridgewaters met at art school, they have two sons, and they live in Cornwall, England.

They have produced more than thirty books to date, including this and the following titles published by STERLING PUBLISHING COMPANY:

- Carving Figureheads & Other Nautical Designs
- Carving Totem Poles & Masks
- Folk Art Woodcarving: 823 Detailed Patterns
- Making Noah's Ark Toys in Wood
- Painted Wood Projects in the Pennsylvania Folk Art Style
- Power Tool Woodcarving
- Traditional Pull-Along Toys in Wood
- Treasury of Woodcarving Designs
- Woodturning Traditional Folk Toys

Books in the Basics Series

- Band Saw Basics
- Cabinetry Basics
- Finishing Basics
- Joinery Basics
- Plane Basics
- Radial Arm Saw Basics
- Router Basics
- Scroll Saw Basics
- Sharpening Basics
- Table Saw Basics
- Toymaking Basics
- Woodcarving Basics